Interview Techniques for UX Practitioners

Interview Techniques for UX Practitioners

UX Practitioners

A User-Centered Design Method

Chauncey Wilson

AMSTERDAM • BOSTON • HEIDELBERG • LONDON
NEW YORK • OXFORD • PARIS • SAN DIEGO
SAN FRANCISCO • SINGAPORE • SYDNEY • TOKYO
Morgan Kaufmann is an imprint of Elsevier

Acquiring Editor: Meg Dunkerley
Development Editor: Heather Scherer
Project Manager: Mohana Natarajan

Morgan Kaufmann is an imprint of Elsevier
225 Wyman Street, Waltham, MA 02451, USA

First published 2014

British Library Cataloguing-in-Publication Data
A catalogue record for this book is available from the British Library

Library of Congress Cataloging-in-Publication Data
A catalog record for this book is available from the Library of Congress

ISBN: 978-0-12-410393-1

For information on all MK publications
visit our website at *www.mkp.com*

This book has been manufactured using Print On Demand technology. Each copy is produced to order and is limited to black ink. The online version of this book will show color figures where appropriate.

Working together
to grow libraries in
developing countries

www.elsevier.com • www.bookaid.org

CONTENTS

Much of the work of user-centered design (UCD) practitioners involves some type of interviewing. Interviewing is used, for example, when you are performing the following tasks:

- Selecting participants for research
- Moderating usability studies
- Briefing and debriefing during usability evaluations
- Conducting focus groups
- Doing phone interviews when you can't afford to travel to a site or bring users to your site
- Gathering information about users, tasks, and workflows in the field
- Performing site visits
- Discussing reactions to storyboards
- Developing scenarios and use cases.

While interviewing is an important skill in our field, many colleagues have little or no formal training in interviewing methods and often learn on the job with limited feedback on the quality of their interviews. What does it take to be a successful interviewer? Kvale (1996) lists 10 criteria for successful interviewers:

- **Knowledgeable:** The interviewer is familiar with the research questions and focus of the interviews and has done some background research into the domain, potential participants, and context of the interview. The interviewer is familiar with at least the basic terminology of the domain.
- **Clear:** The interviewer uses language that is appropriate for the participants and avoids technical jargon and acronyms.
- **Gentle:** The interviewer gives people time to finish their responses without interrupting them and understands that silence and reflection are part of good interviews.
- **Structuring:** The interviewer explains the goals of the interview clearly and asks if the participant has any questions about the topic or procedures.

- **Sensitive:** The interviewer is a good listener and notices things like subtle shifts in tone (e.g., from a normal voice to one that is critical or dubious).
- **Open:** The interviewer is flexible about topics that the participant feels are important when the survey is semi-structured or unstructured.
- **Steering:** The interviewer is clear on the goals of the interview and steers the interview appropriately, especially for semi-structured and unstructured interviews. The interviewer does not go too far off the main topic of the interview except when there is evidence of a new line of inquiry that has great promise.
- **Critical:** The interviewer can challenge the participant gently when inconsistencies emerge during the interview.
- **Remembering:** The interviewer can recall what the participant has been previously stated and bring that information into the interview session. The interviewer also remembers if a question has already been answered and does not re-ask a question that has been fully covered already.
- **Interpreting:** The interview can clarify and extend statements made by the participant without unduly influencing the participant's original meaning.

The chapters in this book will discuss specific ways to meet these criteria and become a successful interviewer.

Chapters 1–3 describe the three basic interview methods: **structured interviews, semi-structured interviews, and unstructured interviews**. These chapters provide best practices and procedures for conducting effective and efficient interviews.

Chapter 4 focuses on **phone interviews** and some of the issues with conducting long-distance interviews, which is becoming more common with remote testing and collaboration technologies (as well as travel limitations). While phone interviews may not be considered as glamorous as focus groups of usability testing, they are a key part of many user research plans because they allow a wide geographic reach at a low cost. Along with the many benefits of phone interviews, there are some pitfalls that practitioners must consider such as the legal issues with recording across state and country borders, memory limitations when asking questions (you can't have as many choices as you would with a written or online questionnaire), and the pacing of the questions.

Chapter 5 covers the **focus group** method. This may seem like an odd choice for a book on interviewing, but a focus group is really a group interview and there are times when you want to take advantage of groups that are visiting or attending conferences. You can plan a focus group or you might (serendipitously) have a group of users available for a short time and use focus group techniques to gather useful information The focus group method is sometimes maligned in our field because we are asking users their opinions about products rather than observing them actually using the products. The focus group method is also susceptible to the "loud participant" bias where one or a few vocal people sway the comments of others, especially if the moderator is not well prepared and experienced. These and other problems of group interviews can be mitigated and you can even combine focus groups with other methods like testing, surveys, and inspections This chapter describes some techniques for making focus groups useful and usable for UCD practitioners.

Chapter 6 focuses on two general issues, sampling and the use of incentives, that are relevant to multiple interview (and other UCD) methods.

Structured Interviews

Alternate Names: Directive interview, researcher-administered survey, standardized interview

Related Methods: Questionnaire, semi-structured interviews, unstructured interviews

OVERVIEW OF STRUCTURED INTERVIEWS

The structured interview is a verbal questionnaire in which the interaction is limited by a script and a fixed set of questions. You might be familiar with structured interviews from those intrusive phone surveys that you get in the evening when you are sitting down to dinner with your family. Just as you are about to partake of a culinary feast, you get a call. Someone introduces himself as part of the "Howard Survey Company," and he wants to ask you "a few" questions. You must decide between eating hot food and taking the survey.

Structured interviews can be conducted in person, over the phone, or through collaboration technologies such as chat. The structured interview has a specific format that interviewers are asked to follow with as little deviation as possible. It uses both closed and open questions to gather information on specific issues but most often asks participants to select a response from a numerical range or set of fixed responses.

Every participant is generally asked the same questions in the same order (or an order prescribed by screening questions). For closed questions, participants answer questions using standardized response categories. Here is a simple example of a closed question with standard response categories:

How would you rate the usability of Product "X"? Very Good, Good, Fair, or Poor

The emphasis on standardization of the questions and responses is to ensure that answers can be reliably grouped and compared.

What if People Don't Give You Standardized Answers?

For the question provided previously about the usability of a product, you might get an answer such as the following: "The usability is pretty good." Does this mean that the usability is "good" or "fair"? Asking the participant what "good" or "fair" means is a bad practice because participants respond differently to response scales with different numbers of items; here, you now have a scale with two items rather than the original four items (Fowler & Mangione, 1990). The appropriate thing to do is to repeat all the response alternatives to make sure the answer is not a function of the interviewer's scale truncation. Repeating the response categories each time can feel awkward, especially if you have a long list of rating scales, but consistent repetition is important for consistency. You might include a note in your script that you will be repeating the scale each time to ensure consistency across all your interviews.

Structured interviews are most appropriate when the product team is aware of the major issues in a project and wants to collect detailed and consistent information about those specific issues. Structured interviews often benefit from the results of previously conducted unstructured or semi-structured interviews that expose the most important issues for users and ranges of reactions to those issues.

WHEN SHOULD YOU USE STRUCTURED INTERVIEWS?

The structured interview is useful for the following:

- Obtaining general information about demographics (e.g., years of experience in a role, gender, education, professional affiliations), behaviors (e.g., "how many times did you call technical support in the past month?"), and relationships (e.g., "who do you have to work with on a major project?").
- Assessing knowledge about a subject. Knowledge questions are used to determine the level of knowledge held by an individual or group of individuals.
- Gathering focused information about stakeholders and their attitudes toward a product, set, or process.
- Asking specific questions after you understand the broad issues of a particular domain, product, or project.
- Collecting uniform data from a large sample of participant and organizations.
- Comparing results across different groups of users on a fixed set of responses. For example, you might want to compare how well various groups of users compare on satisfaction scores.

Structured interviews can last from several minutes (short interviews in malls, airports, or fast-food restaurants) to several hours for in-depth interviews with dedicated participants.

Structured interviews can be used throughout the development cycle (Table 1.1) but are most useful when the goals and major issues of a project are well understood and you know enough to generate a list of expected response categories. The small bar charts in Table 1.1 provide a sense of the overall effort, planning time,

Table 1.1 Method Scorecard for Structured Interviews

Overall Effort Required	Time for Planning and Conducting	Skill and Experience	Supplies and Equipment	Time for Data Analysis
▪▫▫▫	▪▪▫▫	▪▪▪▫	▪▫▫▫	▪▪▫▫

Most Useful During These Phases

Problem Definition	Requirements	Conceptual Design	Detailed Design	Implementation
	✓	✓	✓	✓

skill, resources, and analysis time, required to conduct structured interviews.

STRENGTHS

Structured interviews have the following strengths:

- Relatively untrained interviewers can more easily conduct these interviews than semi-structured or unstructured interviews. Training and interview development is generally less costly than it is for less structured interviews.
- Responses are more reasonably comparable (than less structured interviews) because all interviews are based on the same set of questions and response categories.
- Structured interviews can be done face-to-face, over the telephone, or through video conferencing systems like Microsoft Lync or Skype.
- Data analysis is relatively easy given that most questions have structured responses. You can easily aggregate data and compare data among subgroups.

WEAKNESSES

Structured interviews have the following weaknesses:

- Creating valid and reliable structured questions and responses requires solid background in questionnaire design—something that is often missing from product teams. Developing structured interview questionnaires may seem easy, but it is not.
- If you are not sure you are asking the right questions in your structured interview, you can end up with precise answers to the wrong questions. Structured interviews are most useful when you have conducted earlier studies to understand the domain or problem area of interest.
- Structured interviews require interviewers to behave consistently when reading questions, probing, and recording answers. This is not as easy as it sounds (Fowler & Mangione, 1990). Interviewers can become less consistent as they get tired, start to anticipate answers, or start to use shortcuts.

- The goal of standardization can make it difficult for interviewers to gain rapport with participants. A rigid script doesn't help the interviewer connect well with the participant.
- The structured interview puts participants in a more passive role than semi-structured or unstructured interviewing. Structured interviewing may give participants the impression that the interview team has already made up its mind about what is important.

WHAT DO YOU NEED TO USE STRUCTURED INTERVIEWS?

This section provides a brief description of the basic resources needed to conduct a structured interview.

Personnel, Participants, and Training

Structured interviews require an interviewer, a participant, and optionally, a notetaker for face-to-face interviews. Structured interviews are often conducted by a single person, but they can be conducted using two-person teams where one person conducts the interview, and the other person takes notes, handles the recording equipment, and acts as a memory aid when recording is not allowed (thus allowing the interviewer to focus on the script). If you are planning a large-scale interview study (hundreds of interviews), you will probably hire an interviewing team from a specialized firm to conduct face-to-face or phone interviews.

Structured interviews require training on how to minimize interviewer-related error and be consistent from session to session. The interviewer must be trained to do the following:

- Develop rapport and professional respect in a short period of time.
- Ask questions in exactly the same way across all interviews.
- Use neutral (non-directional) probes.
- Apply appropriate reinforcement during interviews. You might, for example, say something like "This is the kind of information that is very helpful to our study."
- Capture notes verbatim without adding much commentary.
- Be consistent across a wide variety of participants.

Training on these topics includes feedback during pilot interviews with participants and some ongoing feedback and review.

Hardware and Software

No specific hardware or software is required for structured interviews. You can use computer-assisted interviewing (CAI) software or a homegrown interview tool running on a laptop computer or tablet computer. The interview tool should include the initial briefing, questions, skip instructions (notes to skip a question because of an answer on a previous question), notes for the interviewer, prompts, and responses.

Documents and Materials

Documents and materials for structured interviews include the following:

- An interview project plan.
- A letter of introduction that you can send or e-mail to prospective participants and their management (unless you are planning cold calls).
- Informed consent forms that explain the purpose of the study, any risks associated with the interview sessions, an explanation of how the data will be used, and permission for data recordings.
- An easy-to-administer questionnaire. You don't want a questionnaire that the interviewers have trouble reading because the text is too small or the formatting too dense.
- Nondisclosure agreement (NDA) forms if the participants have not already signed a form.
- Some type of database or software for storing and analyzing qualitative data (if you have large amounts of data). You may want to examine data over a period of time or compare it to other sources of data, so some way to store it can be beneficial in the long run. One emerging theme with survey results is that of privacy of personal information. There are laws about how user/customer data are tracked, stored, and distributed. Check with your corporate security office about privacy laws related to "personally identifiable information (PII)." The key point about PII is that you should not store open information that would allow you to identify a single person in a particular context or present results from interviews that might allow someone to identify a particular participant. For example, if you did interviews at a client site and in your report of the interviews, you noted comments from the "lone disabled engineer" you

might be providing enough information for someone to figure out who that disabled engineer was.

- Interview agendas or guides with the general areas that you will cover and potential probing questions.
- Maps and good directions.
- Small gifts or incentives for your hosts and those who you interviewed. See Chapter 6 for more details on intrinsic and extrinsic incentives.

PROCEDURES AND PRACTICAL ADVICE ON STRUCTURED INTERVIEWS

The key issue for planning and conducting structured interviews is to present questions, allowable responses, and neutral probes (e.g., if a participant asks for help, you can have a series of statements that are neutral and consistent such as repeating the question or saying "tell me whatever it means to you") in a consistent manner that does not influence the participant to answer in a particular way. The main goal of the structured interview method is to minimize interviewer-related measurement error (Fowler & Mangione, 1990).

Planning the Structured Interview

When planning a structured interview, follow these steps:

1. **Determine the goals of your structured interview study**. Why are you conducting this structured interview? This is a simple question but one that is sometimes lost when teams decide to "throw together some questions and call some customers or users." Some general goals include:
   a. Collecting specific quantitative (and sometimes qualitative) data from a sample of users and customers.
   b. Comparing the results from this interview to a past interview.
   c. Gathering data to compare across groups.
   d. Answering specific research questions.
   e. Screening candidates for hiring or research studies.

2. **Determine whether you will depend on intrinsic motivation to get people to accept your request for an interview or use some type of extrinsic incentive such as money, software, or gift certificates to increase response rates.** For more details on incentives, see Chapter 6.

3. **List the general questions or hypotheses that you want answered from the interviews.** Structured questionnaires are useful most often when you already have some background from prior research efforts and are relatively certain that you have the "right" set of questions and response categories.

Choosing Open-Ended Versus Closed-Ended Questions for a Structured Interview

In a structured interview, should you use open-ended questions that allow participants to answer questions in their own words rather than closed-ended questions that force participants to choose from a pre-scribed list of answers? A simple example here might be a question about "job titles." Do you let people enter whatever they want, which could be a mix of formal titles (e.g., Senior Interface Designer, Principle UX Designer) with working titles (e.g., Chief UX Evangelist), or do you require participants to check a set of "official" titles? With open-ended questions, you could end up with dozens of titles—some official, some descriptive (e.g., Guru of Design), and some inflated. With a closed-ended question, you may not capture some of the jobs or roles of your participants.

Analyzing open-ended data is time consuming compared to the simple tabulating of rating scales or forced-choice answer categories. The best approach might be to use open-ended questions in pilot or early studies and create closed-ended response categories based on analysis of your open-ended data. Schuman and Presser (1981) conducted a series of experiments comparing open-ended and closed-ended questions. One main finding was that there was little difference in answers from the two types of questions when opened-ended data from pilot studies were used to generate closed-ended response categories.

The simple lesson here is to conduct a pilot study with open-ended responses if you don't know much about how people will answer a particular question. Then derive your fixed responses from an analysis of the open-ended data. If you include open-ended questions in a structured interview, you need to be consistent in how you ask the questions, describe the responses, and ask for clarification. You would not want to add extra editorial comments like "that's a wicked cool job title!"

Table 1.2 Connect Business and Research Goals with Interview Questions		
Business Goal	**Research Goal**	**Question**
Increase the satisfaction of our customers	Measure satisfaction with different aspects of our product	How likely are you to recommend our product to your colleagues using other products?

4. **Create a pool of questions that address the general questions or hypotheses without defining the particular format of the question (e.g., is it a closed or open question; is it a yes/no question).** This pool of general questions is the raw material for your interview questionnaire. List the types of information that you need for each question. For example, for the question "How do people prioritize the work that they perform daily?" you might need to know the following:
   - What is the work that you do?
   - How often do you do this work?
   - What are the consequences of the work?
   - Who assigns the work to you?
   - Is there any official prioritization scheme in your organization (e.g., anything from the director automatically gets a high priority)?

5. **Choose your interview questions from the question pool.** Consider the following criteria:
   - The relevance of each question to the goals of your project. It should be possible to connect each question to a clear business or research goal. If you can't connect each question to a clear goal, then delete it. You might consider creating a matrix (Table 1.2) where you explicitly connect specific business and research goals to questions.
   - The usability of the questions themselves. Questions should be appropriate for your target audience *and* the interviewer.
   - The range of responses to closed and partially closed questions. The number of responses should not tax the cognitive abilities of participants significantly (e.g., don't ask the person to rank 10 items that are presented verbally—that is nearly an impossible task!).

6. **Select the appropriate question and response formats for each question.** Table 1.3 lists response formats for different types of questions.

Table 1.3 Types of Questions and Response Formats Used in Structured Interviews	
Type of Question	**Response Format**
Fill-in-the-blank	Short answers for information such as name, age, and occupation.
Open-ended	No particular response format is used here although the interviewer can indicate what constitutes an adequate answer. The interviewer is to record answers verbatim and probe for clarity to ensure that the answer will be understood during the analysis phase.
Binary (or limited) choices for factual information	Yes/no/does not apply/don't want to answer.
Rating scale	5-point/7-point rating scales with verbal labels.
Ranking	Rank a number of items along a particular dimension such as frequency, importance, and interest. Ranking questions must be kept simple.
Choose from a list of unordered choices	Here you ask the participant to choose one or more items from a list that has no particular order. For example, you might ask a person "Which of the seven statements below best describes. . .?" The user is asked to choose a single answer.

Written Aids for Participants

In face-to-face interviews, you might provide your participants with a written aid that has the question and response categories for complex questions with multiple answers. For example, you might have cards for complex questions or questions with a long list of alternatives. If you use written aids, make sure that the text is large enough to be legible to participants from all age groups.

You can also use written aids for phone or online audio interviews. You can e-mail or fax a set of questions to the participants so they can think about the answers before you call and then use the list of questions to reduce memory load.

7. **Determine the best order of questions.** This is not an easy task, and the research is mixed with regard to general ordering principles (Dillman, 2009; Weller, 1998). Here are some general suggestions for ordering questions:
   - Use a funnel approach where you start with broad general questions and then proceed to more specific questions. Weller (1998) notes that asking specific questions first might bias answers to more general questions. For example, if you were designing a product satisfaction questionnaire, asking people about all the problems with a product early in the survey might bias general

questions (e.g., "Would you recommend this product to another colleague?") that are located at the end of the survey.

- Avoid difficult, threatening, or emotionally laden questions at the beginning of the interview. The first few questions should be ones that are relevant to most people, engaging, and not too difficult or threatening.
- Avoid asking basic demographic questions (e.g., "What is your age? How large is your company? Where do you work?") at the beginning unless they are required for screening purposes (e.g., you might want to screen for experience and ask different questions for novices versus experts). Ask most demographic questions at the end of the interview. If your participants have answered most of your substantive questions, they will very likely answer a set of demographic questions at the end of the interview.
- Organize questions by topic and indicate the topic when you start a new set of questions.
- Before asking questions that might be viewed as personal, remind the participant that this information is confidential and won't be identified in any way on the final report.
- Have several colleagues review the order of the questions to see if the answers to a particular question might bias the next question.

8. **Create the interviewer script and questionnaire with a focus on making it clear and easy for the interviewer.** Define the formatting conventions that you will use for your interview script and questionnaire. Consider conventions for the following:

  - **Text that is only for the interviewer.** The interviewer may have notes about skipping questions depending on answers to previous questions or a list of standard probes for a question. These interviewer-only instructions might, for example, be in ALL UPPERCASE to clearly distinguish private instructions from text that will be read to the participant. Here is an example:
    IF PARTICIPANT ANSWERS "NO" TO QUESTION 5, THEN SKIP TO QUESTION 9.
  - **Text where the interviewer has to decide between exact choices.** For example, if the person is interviewing people in their homes about their use of mobile devices, the interviewer may have a

place where he can use the word, "husband," the word, "wife," or the word "partner," in a question depending on the participant's relationship. Optional (but exact) text can be placed in parentheses so the interviewer uses the same words consistently: (husband/wife/partner).

- **Text that is read to the participant.** This text includes an introduction to the interview, the actual questions, and the responses. This text can be in normal mixed-case format.

9. **Review the wording of all questions and response categories, and make sure they can be understood in the same way by all participants.** Here are some general guidelines for ensuring common understanding of questions and response categories (Converse & Presser, 1986; Fowler, 1995; Payne, 1951):

- **Use common "spoken" language for face-to-face and phone interviews.** It may be better to violate conventions that are common in written documents than to force participants to listen to formal language. For example, in an interview in English, you can use contractions more freely than you would in a formal report or academic publication.

- **Make questions as specific as possible.** Specific questions have two advantages: they can assist recall of events, and they are more likely to be interpreted in the same way.

- **Avoid abstractions that might be simple for you, but complex for your participants.** Converse and Presser (1986) describe a question that involved the concept of "comparative rate of change" and note that this is a concept more suited to a calculus class than a structured survey of the general populace. The concept of "usability debt" (old usability problems that have not been fixed over a long period of time), for example, might be quite useful in prioritizing problems within your product team, but too abstract a concept for a structured interview question.

- **Consider whether you need to provide a frame of reference for particular terms.** For example, if you are asking a question about "usability," you might want to define what it means in your context. Many usability practitioners can't agree on what this word means, so should we expect our users to understand? Probably not. Similarly, if you were asking about a person's "workgroup," you might provide a succinct definition of that term.

●●●
_____

When you define terms in interviews (e.g., "usability"), keep in mind that the definition may constrain the responses of the participant. If you want the broadest range of responses, you might tell participants, if they ask, that a term "means whatever they think it means." If you were doing an unstructured interview (Chapter 3), you might ask questions that get at the participant's understanding of a term like "usability." In a structured interview, you may simply have a definition that you read to everyone while trying to avoid providing any additional cues (which is hard in phone and face-to-face structured interviews).

_____

- **Provide the participant with a clear idea of what an adequate answer is for questions.** For example, if you were interested in how long a person had worked in a particular job, you would not ask the question "How long have your worked in your current job?" because that opens the possibility of different ways of answering such as "Quite a while," "Many years," "36.5 months," and "Since the group was organized." A better question such as "How many years have you worked in your job?" provides a cue about how to answer the question. Whenever possible, have someone who is an expert at survey and questionnaire design help you design your questions and responses, or at least review them for question and response problems.

10. **Pilot test the entire interview process from meeting your hosts through packing up your equipment and materials, thanking your participant and hosts, and leaving the site.** You can start with a focus group or walkthrough of the interview to eliminate any major issues and then run several pilot tests with potential participants to refine your interview materials and process. Consider the following during your pilot testing:
    - **Pacing of the interview.** A good interviewer is aware of pacing and adjusts, within limits, to a pace that is comfortable for the participant and that allows adequate time to think about the question and responses. Some interviewers may increase their pace as they gain experience with a particular survey which could discourage participants from thinking about the question and lead to reduced data quality (Fowler & Mangione, 1990; Olson & Peytchev, 2007).
    - **Consistency of the interviewers.** You might videotape several interviews with a small sample of participants and examine whether the

interviewers read questions exactly, modified the questions in a way that was very minor, or changed the meaning of the question or responses significantly. If you don't have time for videotaping and peer review, just ask a colleague to listen to or view an interview and give you quick feedback on interview consistency.

- **Responses to both common and rare interview events.** Consider how the interviewer handled nonresponses, interruptions, and answers that were not clear. One useful exercise is to have different colleagues role-play "difficult" participants and provide some early practice on how to handle unusual or unexpected responses.

Use the pilot testing to get a good estimate of how long the interview will last. If you are interviewing people over the phone, you need to pilot test over the phone. (See Chapter 4 for specific information on phone interviews.)

11. **Develop an introduction for your interview.** Develop an introductory letter or verbal introduction that describes the goals for your study, how the data will be used, how long the interview will last, and the possible impact of the data on the participant. Keep in mind that this introduction is meant to create trust between interviewer and participant.

12. **Recruit participants who meet your screening criteria.** See Chapter 6 for a discussion of sampling approaches.

13. **Determine where you will interview your participants.** This might seem like a minor point, but for face-to-face interviews, you need to consider the following aspects of the setting:
    - Is there enough privacy for the participant to feel comfortable?
    - Are there any distractions that will compromise the interview?
    - How difficult is it for the participant of a face-to-face interview to get to your location?

14. **Create and assemble any forms or documents that you need, including these:**
    - Screeners and letters that you use to recruit participants.
    - An informed consent form.
    - An NDA.
    - Any receipts for compensation.

Training Your Interview Team on How to Standardize the Structured Interview

A cardinal rule for structured interviews is that individual interviewers are consistent across interviews and that multiple interviewers are consistent with each other in their interview techniques. Robson (2002) and Fowler and Mangione (1990) list some important aspects of interview consistency:

- **Appearance.** Dress consistently across your interviews. If there are multiple interviewers, discuss what is acceptable attire for the interviews and wear clothes that fall within the acceptable range. In many situations, "business casual" would be appropriate. Avoid buttons, pins, or accessories that indicate religious, political, or personal philosophies.
- **Familiarity with the questionnaire/interview schedule.** Know the questions, responses, and probes well. Practice mock interviews and have colleagues observe and give you feedback on your interview techniques.
- **Read questions exactly as they are written.** This is a cardinal rule for structured interviews. In addition to reading the words as they are written, make sure that your style of reading doesn't emphasize particular words in a question or a particular response for a closed-ended question. The best way to improve on consistent reading of questions and responses is to audiotape or videotape pilot sessions and have several colleagues review the pilots and note whether there are any obvious biases. In corporate environments, you may not have time to practice and get feedback from multiple colleagues so you might simply interview a colleague and then do a brief retrospective about any reading issues. As you gain experience with the interview, consider if you are altering your delivery or adding little "helper phrases" for questions where you find participants struggling a bit.
- **Probes.** If the participant's answer is not clear or complete enough for open-ended questions in a structured interview, use neutral probes (statements that don't suggest an answer or direction to a response) that will not affect the content of the participant's answer. For example, you might use a set of neutral problems such as the following:
  - "Tell me more about that."
  - "What do you mean?"
  - "Do you have anything else you want to add?"
- **Recording answers.** The interviewer should not paraphrase or abbreviate what the participant says. Answers should be recorded exactly as they were stated by the participant. Here is where it is useful to have a recording device, although many times organizational concerns about privacy and security will make it difficult to use a recording device.

- **Personal biases.** Particular behaviors or speech patterns of interviewers can affect the participant's response. Even such simple feedback as saying "Great!" or "That's really good feedback [to an open-ended question]" can affect the participant's responses to subsequent questions. How to respond to answers is something that interview teams should discuss during planning.

Conducting the Structured Interview

Structured interviews can be done in person, over the telephone, or via the Internet using collaboration and recording technologies. This section will describe the general steps for conducting a structured interview.

1. **Brief the person about the reasons and goals for the interview, and be prepared for common questions.** The participants must understand the purpose of the interview and how they can contribute through their participation. There are some common questions that participants might ask regarding the interview. It is useful to have a Frequently Asked Questions (FAQ) document listing and answering questions such as the following that the participants might ask:
   - Where did you get my name?
   - What is the goal of this study?
   - Who is the sponsor of the study?
   - Who will use the information from this study?
   - Will anyone know that I was interviewed?
   - Do I have to answer all your questions?
   - Where will the data be reported?
   - Can I have a copy of the report when your study is over?
2. **Establish rapport with the person and establish a positive (but not overly friendly) tone for the interview.** There is a delicate balance here because you need to establish a positive tone without attempting to befriend the participant. You want the interview to be professional rather than personal, so do not volunteer too many personal details about yourself—don't mention pets, cars, recent movies, politics, or religion! Some techniques for establishing rapport include:
   - Reassure that you won't be asking anyone to buy anything.
   - A bit of small talk not related to the purpose of the structured interview.
   - A positive demeanor with visual cues of friendliness like smiling.
   - Eye contact with the participant.

- A warm voice and verbal interactions that are not too rushed.
- Introductory questions that are easy to answer and nonthreatening.
3. **Be clear about the guidelines for the interview.** For example, you should indicate that you are a neutral interviewer and can't reveal details or your own opinions about something or chat about a topic. In a classic study about behavior of interviewers, Cannell, Fowler, and Marquis (1968) found that about 50% of what went on during structured interviews had little to do with the instructions, questions, responses, or probes—it was just idle chatter between the interviewer and participant, which dealt with the topic at hand but still reduced the degree of standardization considerably.
4. **Set a reasonable pace for the interview.** If you go too fast, you may get quick but incomplete and inaccurate answers. You should consider pacing earlier in the planning when you conduct your pilot test and plan the amount of time required for an interviewed based on a moderate pace that doesn't feel rushed.
5. **If you have multiple face-to-face interviews at a single site, try to meet with all the people you plan to interview in a group at the beginning of the day and give everyone an overview of your general plans (e.g., you will be audiotaping, the interview will take about an hour).** If you can set up this "group introduction," you can save time (you don't have to repeat the introductory information for each person), make sure that there is a schedule set up for the day's interviews, start building professional rapport, and, if appropriate, have everyone fill out any required forms.
6. **When you meet each participant (in a face-to-face interview), ask where you should sit. If you need to set up any equipment, make sure that you don't interfere with anything in the participant's space.** Consider whether privacy is more important than being in the participant's actual work space. If the interview is potentially sensitive, consider going to a more private space.
7. **Review the interview process briefly with each participant (this should be outlined as part of your script).** Things that you should mention to the participant include the following:
   - A brief description of the interview topic and goals, the stages in the interview process, recording, and ethical issues, and comments about prompting and also cutting short some discussions to ensure that there is good coverage.
   - How long the interview will take.

- What you will do if the person has to answer the phone or leave momentarily (shut off all recording equipment and offer to step away).
- What you will be doing with the data and (if you plan to send anything back to the participant) how they can get a summary of the results. If you do not plan to let the participant (or the managers who arranged the interview) see any data, be very careful what you say about the results. Remind the participant that the data will be confidential and describe how you will keep it that way.

Remember that the participant is doing you a favor, so this introduction is important for making the interview a pleasant experience.

8. **During the main part of the interview, follow the interview script as closely as possible and ask the same questions of all participants.** The goal here is to be as consistent as possible across interviews and interviewers.

9. **When the interview is over, signal a clear end to the conversation by thanking the participant, putting away note-taking materials, and turning off any recording devices.** If you have promised any payment or other compensation for the interview, give it to the participant, have him or her sign a receipt if necessary, and (if appropriate) ask if it is OK to contact the participant if any questions emerge during the data analysis. Thank the participant for his or her time. If you made any commitments, review them with the participant before you go, and if you misspoke about anything, clear it up immediately.

After the Structured Interview Session

When your interview has concluded, follow these steps:

1. **Write up your notes in a summary form as soon as possible after each interview.** Schedule time to enter the data from the structured interview into a spreadsheet, database, or common data form after each interview or at the end of the day.

2. **Make sure that you have all your forms, tapes, and materials marked with a code for that interview so you don't waste time when you begin your data analysis trying to figure out which notes go with which participants.** If the participant gave you any artifacts, label them with a code for the interview.

3. **Make sure that you back up (and possibly write protect) any audio or video files.**

VARIATIONS AND EXTENSIONS TO STRUCTURED INTERVIEWS

There are no significant variations or extensions to the structured interview method.

MAJOR ISSUES WITH STRUCTURED INTERVIEWS

The next section of this chapter describes some major issues that you need to consider if you are planning structured interviews.

Low Popularity

Structured interviews are probably the least popular type of interview (compared to semi-structured and unstructured interviews) because they force the participants to answer many questions with a rigid set of answers. Here are some things you can do to make structured interviews a more positive activity for participants:

- Be clear about the ground rules for the interview; for example, let the participant know that you are not permitted to further discuss of the questions.
- Don't give the impression you are rushing through the interview.
- Try to arrange a time that is convenient for the participant.

Sensitive Topics

If you are using structured interviews, be sensitive to questions that might tend to do the following:

- Incriminate
- Show someone in a bad light
- Ask for sensitive personal information
- Require the participant to say something against organizational policy

Questions about factors that affect an participant's performance, for example, might be viewed as threatening. Questions dealing with how people interact with coworkers can also bring up "office animosities" that people might find uncomfortable talking about in an interview setting. The same issue can come up with less structured interviewing techniques, but those methods allow interviewers some discretion while the structured approach is supposed to be applied consistently. So if there are sensitive questions, interviewers are expected to ask them of everyone and press on regardless of signals of discomfort.

Data Quality: Types of Questions That May Lead to Poor Data Quality

Fowler (1995) warns interview creators to focus on firsthand experiences and advises against the following:

- Asking about secondhand information.
- Asking hypothetical questions. There may be occasions where hypothetical questions can be used, but generally they should be avoided.
- Asking about causality. People are often very poor at "why" questions and may tell more than they know about why something happened (Nisbett & Wilson, 1977).
- Asking about solutions to complex problems (there could be exceptions here if you are talking to a technical architect or the chief designer).

CONCLUSIONS

Structured interviews are used to gather data in a highly organized way. The data from structured interviews are generally easy to code and analyze. Structured interviews can be conducted face-to-face, by phone, or through collaboration software. Interviewers must adhere to strict rules for asking questions and presenting responses to ensure consistency. This chapter provides general procedures for planning and conducting structured interviews and also provides tips and notes about how to have successful structured interviews.

CHAPTER 2

Semi-Structured Interviews

Alternative Names: Focused interview, qualitative research interview

Related Methods: Focus group, structured interview, unstructured interview

OVERVIEW OF SEMI-STRUCTURED INTERVIEWS

A semi-structured interview combines predefined questions like those used in structured interviews (see Chapter 1) with the open-ended exploration of an unstructured interview (see Chapter 3). Interviewers using the semi-structured interview approach generally follow a document called an interview guide or interview schedule that includes the following:

* An introduction to the purpose and topic of the interview
* A list of topics and questions to ask about each topic
* Suggested probes and prompts
* Closing comments.

The general goal of the semi-structured interview is to gather systematic information about a set of central topics, while also allowing some exploration when new issues or topics emerge.

Semi-structured interviews are used when there is some knowledge about the topics or issues under investigation, but further details are still needed. Semi-structured interviews can be based on topics, issues, and questions that emerged from unstructured interviews or other sources of information.

Semi-structured interviews allow discretion on the number and order of predefined questions posed to the participant (unlike the structured interview described in Chapter 1 where interviewers are required to follow a detailed script with little latitude for asking emergent questions or varying from the script). This type of interview involves the use of both open-ended and closed-ended questions and can provide both quantitative and qualitative data.

WHEN SHOULD YOU USE SEMI-STRUCTURED INTERVIEWS?

You can use semi-structured interviewing to do the following:

* Gather facts, attitudes, and opinions.
* Gather data on topics where the interviewer is relatively certain that the relevant issues have been identified, but still provide users with

the opportunity to raise new issues that are important to them through open-ended questions.

- Gather data when you cannot observe behavior directly because of timing, hazards, privacy, or other factors. You might, for example, use a structured interview approach to gather data on the usability of Army command and control systems.
- Understand user goals.
- Gather information about tasks, task flow, and work artifacts such as job aids, forms, best practices documents, workflow diagrams, signs, equipment, photographs, and posters.

Interviews and Artifacts

When you visit a home, work, or recreational site to conduct interviews, you are often trying to understand the culture. Each site is filled with artifacts—objects that have work or cultural significance—that can help you understand users and their environments. A flowchart of a company's development process, for example, can be the stimulus for an interview and helps the participant to tell a powerful story. Artifacts, such as collages or workflow diagrams, can be generated and discussed as part of an interview. Workplace artifacts are often associated with ethnographic interviews but are also useful in semi-structured and unstructured interviews where the interviewer has freedom to explore new paths and ask questions about particular artifacts.

- Gather data on complex issues where probing and clarification of answers are required.

Semi-structured interviews can obviously vary in length from several minutes to several hours. Interviews that are too long may reduce the pool of qualified participants who don't want to give up valuable work time; interviews that are too short may not provide enough time to establish rapport and cover the topic in sufficient depth. Consider arranging semi-structured interviews that last from half an hour to two hours (including introductions, building rapport, and winding down at the end) unless you know that the participants are quite dedicated and willing to give up more time (Robson, 2002, p. 273).

If you are doing interviews in environments where people are in a rush (airports, fast food restaurants, and city streets), your interview might use mostly closed-ended questions with a limited number of choices and a few short open-ended questions that are relatively easy to answer. Semi-structured interviews can be used during any phase of product development (Table 2.1). The small bar charts in Table 2.1 provide a sense of the overall effort, planning time, skill, resources, and analysis time required to conduct semi-structured interviews.

STRENGTHS

Semi-structured interviews have the following strengths:

- May uncover previously unknown issues (in contrast to a structured interview).
- Address complex topics through probes and clarification.
- Ensure that particular points are covered with each participant and also allow users and interviewers to raise additional concerns and issues.
- Provide a mechanism for redirecting conversations that digress too far from the main topic.
- Provide some flexibility for interviewers and also allows some broad comparisons across interviews.
- Require less training time than unstructured interviews because the interviewer has a set of specific questions available as a starting point.
- Can be conducted by an outside consulting company because there is a base set of questions (although you should research any external interviewing organization to ensure that they are competent at interviewing, data analysis, and interpretation).

WEAKNESSES

Semi-structured interviews have the following weaknesses:

- There can be an "interviewer effect" where the background, the sex, the age, and other demographics influence how much information people are willing to reveal in an interview (Denscombe, 2010). If you (a usability practitioner with a background in human–computer interaction) were interviewing a structural engineer about work practices, your lack of engineering background might influence how much detail the engineer provided and how much he/she trusted you to understand his/her work practice.

Table 2.1 Method Scorecard for Semi-Structured Interviews

Overall Effort Required	Time for Planning and Conducting	Skill and Experience	Supplies and Equipment	Time for Data Analysis
(rating scale)	(rating scale)	(rating scale)	(rating scale)	(rating scale)

Most Useful During These Phases

Problem Definition	Requirements	Conceptual Design	Detailed Design	Implementation
✓	✓	✓	✓	✓

- Some training and experience are required so that interviewers do not put words into the participant's mouth.
- Interviewers can give cues that might guide the participants into a particular answer.
- Consistency among interviewers is required. Too much flexibility among interviewers might make comparisons difficult. If you have multiple interviewers, consider training the group about how much flexibility they have in probing existing questions or asking new ones.
- The mixture of quantitative and qualitative data that results can be time-consuming to analyze.
- The findings of semi-structured interviews might be hard to generalize because different interviewers may ask some different questions.

WHAT DO YOU NEED TO USE SEMI-STRUCTURED INTERVIEWS?

This section provides a brief description of the basic resources needed to conduct a semi-structured interview.

Personnel, Participants, and Training

Semi-structured interviews are often best conducted using two-person teams where one person conducts the interview and the other person takes notes, handles the recording equipment and acts as a memory aid when recording is not allowed. A dedicated notetaker may not always be available because of funding. If you include a dedicated notetaker, that person should have familiarity with the domain, terminology, and product to make note-taking easier and more accurate. If you cannot record the interview and have no one to take notes, give yourself time between interviews to fill in what you remember but didn't have time to write down during the session.

Ganging Up on the Participant

While two-person interview teams can make the interview somewhat easier, having two people for face-to-face interviews might intimidate the participant, especially if there is any sensitivity to the interview. If the interviews are sensitive, consider having one person to conduct the interview and use an audio recorder to capture details that the interviewer might not be able to catch with manual note-taking.

Training for semi-structured interviews should include the following topics:

- How to write an interview guide.
- How to probe for more detail using neutral prompts that do not suggest an answer to the participant.

●●●

Make a List of Neutral Prompts and Practice Using Them

Many UCD activities call for the use of neutral (nonleading and nondirective) prompts such as these:

"Tell me about..."
"Could you explain a bit more what you meant by...?"
"How do you feel about...?"
"Could you describe...?"

You might find it useful to keep a list of good prompts and include them in the interview guide or even on a notecard that can be used as a cognitive aid for participants during a set of interviews.

- How to deal with silences and how to cut off answers that are not providing anything new.
- How to use verbal prompts to aid the participant's memory.
- How to control body language so that you convey interest without introducing the opinions of the interviewer.
- How to take notes if you don't have help and can't record the interview.
- How to be sensitive to the ethics of the interview. The interviewer should be sensitive to ethical issues involving privacy, sensitive topics, and confidentiality of the data (Bryman, 2004).

Hardware and Software

Semi-structured interviews can benefit from audio or video recorders so you have a complete record of the interview. Digital cameras can be useful for documenting the physical environment and any artifacts that are important to the study topic. If you plan to conduct a large number of interviews (or have large amounts of open-ended data from surveys or other UCD methods), consider using specialized qualitative data analysis tools such as ATLAS.ti, QSR NVivo, THE ETHNOGRAPH, or HyperRESEARCH. Note that these tools are not ones that you pick up quickly. They all require training and practice and may take weeks or months to master.

Documents and Materials

Documents and materials for semi-structured interviews include the following:

- An interview project plan that describes the goals of the study, the recruiting plan, background on the companies and people you are going to visit, the general topics that are of interest, guidelines for interviewers, and the data collection and analysis plan. The level of detail depends on the magnitude of the study, but even small studies can benefit from a project plan.
- A letter of introduction that you can send or email to perspective participants and their management.
- Informed consent forms that explain the purpose of the study, any risks associated with the interview sessions, how the data will be used, and permission for data recordings.
- NDAs are required if the participants have not already signed a form. Check with your legal office on your company's NDA policies. For example, some people may not have the authority to sign an NDA (you might need someone at the director or higher level to do so).
- Some types of database or software are required for storing and analyzing qualitative data (if you have large amounts of data). You may want to examine data over a period of time or compare it to other sources of data, so some way to store it can be beneficial in the long run.
- Interview agendas or guides with the general areas that you will cover and potential probing questions.
- Maps and good directions.
- Small gifts or incentives for your hosts and those you will interview.

PROCEDURES AND PRACTICAL ADVICE ON SEMI-STRUCTURED INTERVIEWS

This section provides a brief description of the basic resources needed to conduct a semi-structured interview.

Planning and Developing the Semi-Structured Interview

To plan and develop a semi-structured interview, follow these steps:

1. **Determine the goals or research focus of your semi-structured interview.** Why are you doing this study? General goals of semi-structured interviews can include the following:
   - Exploring a particular topic, problem, or issue
   - Understanding how a process or function works

- Understanding how particular groups in an organization work together
- Determining what is efficient and inefficient about particular workflows
- Gathering background material for creating personas, task models, or other artifacts
- Testing ideas or hypotheses from other sources
- Confirming (or discomfirming) results from other methods.

2. **Develop a list of general questions that you want to ask during the interview.** Semi-structured interviews have some "standard" questions as well as *ad hoc* questions that are prompted by the respondent. Here are some example questions that can apply to many user or customer interviews (Goodwin, 2009; Hackos & Redish, 1998):
   - What is your background and your role in your organization?
   - What is a description of a typical day/week/month at your job?
   - What do you do with a product (function or service)?
   - What are the problems with this product (function, process, or service)?
   - What are the best things about this product (function, process, or service)?
   - Please list two to three things that you like best about this (function, process, or service).
   - Please list two to three things that you dislike best about this (function, process, or service).
   - What tools, software, or hardware do you use to accomplish your goals? How often do you use these tools?
   - What are the primary outputs of your work? Can you show me some examples?
   - What are the major tasks that you need to complete successfully to accomplish your goals?
   - What are the busiest times of the year?
   - Can you give me a specific example?
   - What factors were involved in choosing this tool (function, process, or service)?
   - How does your company measure success?

3. **Develop your interview guide with the general questions and basic script for the interview**. Table 2.2 is an outline of a sample interview guide. Following are some basic guidelines for developing questions for the interview guide:
   - Avoid the tendency to add "interesting" questions that do not relate to a research goal. Ensure that each question is relevant to

Table 2.2 Rough Outline of a Semi-Structured Interview Guide

Activity	Comments/Questions	Approximate Time
Introduction	Brief the participant. Introduce self. Explain goals of interview. Review interview method, use of data, confidentiality, and so on.	10 min

Structured topics	Topic 1: Background
	    Question 1a
	      Probe 1
	      Probe 2
	      Probe 3
	Topic 2: Context of Work
	    Question 2a
	      Probe 1
	      Probe 2
	    Question 2b
	      Probe 1
	Topic 3: Use of Product
	    Question 3a
	      Probe 1
	Topic N: Additional topics
		40 min

General questions and open dialogue with participant		30 min
Closing comments and completion of any paperwork (receipts, final questionnaire, etc.)		10 min

the goals or hypotheses of your project. It should be possible to connect each question to a clear business or research goal. If you can't connect a question to a clear goal, then delete it.

- Use language that is appropriate for your participants.

Adapt Your Language to Match the Participant

As you conduct your interviews, you will learn about technical terms and phrases that are part of the language of the group you are investigating. Consider incorporating that language into the unstructured aspect of your interviews. If, for example, you hear people consistently using a particular word that you weren't familiar with, you might ask what it means and use it in your interview. Be sure you understand what new terms mean before you use them so that you don't look foolish. Knowing some of the terms of your users can enhance your credibility and help build rapport.

- Avoid questions that are overly long or complex. You can use probes to get more details and clarify responses.

- Don't ask double questions such as "How would you describe the usability and reliability of the new software?" Break questions like this into two questions.
- Do not tax the cognitive abilities of the participant significantly with the range of responses to closed and partially closed questions (e.g., don't ask the person to rank and order 10 items that are presented verbally). If you have questions with response categories that may tax the participant's cognitive abilities, consider putting the question and response categories on a card and hand the card to the participant.
- Review the question order for obvious biases and sensitivities. You may not want to ask a threatening initial question that might influence later responses.
- Listen closely. Interviewers should be trained to be good listeners. Good listeners have the following characteristics:
  - They don't jump in too quickly when a participant is talking.
  - They balance neutrality with motivation. Avoid obviously biased prompts but provide some general reinforcement for the participant.

4. **Recruit participants who meet your screening criteria.**

Tip

Be careful about overrecruiting from your favorite companies. You can wear out your welcome if you keep coming back or you might miss problems that your not-so-favorite customers are having.

5. **Create and assemble any forms or documents that you need, including the following:**
   a. The interview guide with opening remarks, topics and questions, probes, and closing statements.
   b. Screeners and letters that you use to recruit participants.
   c. An informed consent form if required. An informed consent spells out the purpose of the study, the rights of the participant, and any physical or mental stress associated with the study.
   d. An NDA, if necessary. An NDA lists the rules for disclosure of information learned during a study. Some organizations combine the informed consent form and NDA while others keep them separate. If you discuss upcoming development activity, you

may need to have your participants sign an NDA. Conversely, you may have to sign an NDA for each organization you visit if the interviews deal with any sensitive information about your customers or their clients.

    e. Any receipts for compensation. If, for example, you are using Amazon gift certificates, which can be considered as cash, you may ask a person to sign a paper receipt or electronically acknowledge receiving the gift certificate. See Chapter 6 for more details on the use of incentives.

6. **If you are visiting different companies, prepare a briefing memo that describes each company, how the company uses your product, what main issues the company faces, and the agenda for the day.** Also include the names of the participants, their locations, their phone numbers, and a brief note about their role with the product of interest.

7. **Your first few minutes with the participant are likely to set the stage for the success of your interview.** Work on those first few minutes in pilot interviews and keep in mind that the first impressions of the interviewer can be critical to success. An interviewer must be calm, confident, credible, knowledgeable, flexible, and professional—without being arrogant.

8. **Pilot test the entire interview process from meeting your hosts through packing up your equipment and materials, thanking your participant and hosts, and leaving the site.** Refine the process and materials based on the pilot testing. Use the pilot testing to get a good estimate of how long the interview will last.

Conducting the Semi-Structured Interview

To conduct the semi-structured interview, follow these steps:

1. **If possible, meet with all the people you plan to interview at a particular location at the beginning of the day and give the group of participants an overview of your general plans (e.g., you will be audiotaping, the interview will take about an hour, etc.).** If you can set up this "group introduction," you can save time (you don't have to repeat the material for each person), make sure that there is a schedule setup for the day's interviews, start building rapport, and, if appropriate, have everyone fill out any required forms.

Emotion, Body Language, and Self-Disclosure

Be aware of expressions of support, sympathy, joy, anger, and other emotions. In contrast to structured interviews, you may need to show some emotion during the interview (expressing sympathy when the person describes a particularly bad incident with a product) to gain trust and show interest, but avoid any expressions of emotion that might induce participants to tell you "what you want to hear."

Consider carefully your body language during interviews. Are you showing approval or disapproval with facial expressions or changes in posture? A useful training exercise is to set up some interviews where you videotape the interviewer (if you have the equipment, you can tape both the interviewer and participant and use a split screen) and then have several observers review the tape and critique the interviewer on the following:

- Vocal and facial tics or extreme displays of emotion
- Loaded and biased questions
- Transitions between questions
- Ability to get participants to either expand on or curtail their discussions
- Appropriate pauses, interruptions, and listening skills.

Avoid talking too much about yourself. The participant might try to guess what kind of answers you expect. There is a fine line here because some self-disclosure can lead to trust, but too much may lead to biased answers.

---

2. **When you meet each respondent, ask them where you should sit.** If you need to set up any equipment, make sure that you don't interfere with anything in the participant's space. Consider whether privacy is more important than being in the participant's actual work space. If the interview is potentially sensitive, consider going to a more private space such as a conference room or even a remote area of a cafeteria.

3. **Review the interview process briefly with each participant (this should be outlined as part of your script).** Mention the following to the participant:

    a. A brief description of the interview topic and goals, the stages in the interview process, recording and ethical issues, and comments about prompting and also cutting short some discussions to ensure that there is good coverage.

    b. The amount of time that is allocated to the interview.

   c. What you will do if the person has to answer the phone or leave momentarily (shut off all recording equipment and offer to step away).

   d. What you will be doing with the data and (if you plan to send anything back to the participant) how they can get a summary of the results. If you do not plan to let the participant (or the managers who arranged the interview) see any data, be very careful what you say about the results. Remind the participant that the data will be confidential and describe how you will keep it that way.

Remember that the participant is doing you a favor, so this introduction is important for making the interview a pleasant experience.

4. **Begin the interview with some warm-up or introductory questions that are easy, nonthreatening, and relevant.** It is generally important to gather some background on the participants and also to understand the context in which they are using a product or service at the beginning of the interview.

5. **During the main part of the interview, you will begin with the questions on the interview schedule that you want everyone to answer and then ask the remaining questions.** Modify or expand these questions as needed depending on the responses of the participant.

6. **Signal a clear end to the conversation by thanking the participant, putting away note-taking materials, and turning off any recording devices.** If you have promised any payment or other compensation for the interview, give it to the participant, have him or her sign a receipt, if necessary, and ask if it is okay to contact the participant if any questions occur during the data analysis and interpretation.

After the Semi-Structured Interview Session

After the interview, follow these steps:

1. **After you put away your notes and shut off any recording systems to signal the end of the interview, there is a good chance that your participant will engage you in some post-interview conversation that has some valuable nuggets of information or insight, or you may have some reflections immediately after the interview.** Bryman (2004) recommends that you don't switch off the recorder as the interview winds down. Keep recording until the last possible moment. Make brief notes on the participant's comments and your reflections

before you move on to the next interview. According to Bryman, things that you might consider noting include the following:

- A description of the location and setting with a focus on any aspect of the setting that might have affected the conversation between the interviewer and participant. Were you interviewing the person in a cubicle, a private office, or the cafeteria?
- A description about how the interview went. Were you nervous? Was the participant nervous?
- Was there anything in the area that might have affected the interview? For example, was there a manager hovering nearby?
- Was there anything about the interview that was out of the ordinary or that you might want to let others know about?

2. **After each individual interview, collate and mark all your materials (notes, tapes, forms, artifacts, etc.) clearly.** If you are working with a team, meet everyone who has conducted daily interviews and walk through how well things went and analyze if there are any major issues that need to be dealt with before the next set of interviews (from simple things such as correcting a typo on the informed consent form to adding questions to the interview).

3. **Schedule sufficient time between interviews to make some general notes, including questions and issues that you might want to bring up with the next participant.** If you had a colleague serve as notetaker, you might review the session together.

VARIATIONS AND EXTENSIONS TO THE SEMI-STRUCTURED INTERVIEW METHOD

The following section describes variations and extensions to the semi-structured interview method.

Building Work Models Through Multiple Interviews with One or More Experts

Semi-structured interviews can be used to build models that incorporate the objects and processes of a system. One approach to building work models is to interview a number of experts and use the combined results to create a work model that can be refined using additional interviews or other methods. Wood (1997) suggests an alternative approach based on repeated semi-structured interviews with a single expert.

Wood conducted a set of interviews with a single expert to understand how telecommunications equipment was ordered at Brigham Young University. After each interview with this expert, he created an updated version of the model and then conducted another semi-structured interview with the same expert.

This process of *interview—refine—interview* continued until Wood felt that the interviews had yielded a comprehensive model of the ordering process. This model was then shown to other stakeholders who were interviewed regarding their specific perspectives on the process. Feedback from these additional stakeholders was used to refine the model until they were satisfied with the composite work model. This approach of iterative semi-structured interviews with a single expert assumes that the expert has a broad understanding of the work process and can provide information that leads to a good work model prototype.

MAJOR ISSUES WITH SEMI-STRUCTURED INTERVIEWS

The following section describes some major issues that you need to consider if you are planning semi-structured interviews.

Putting Participants at Ease and Making Them Feel Comfortable in Your Presence

You can do some basic things to make your participants comfortable during an interview (Goodwin, 2009; Hackos & Redish, 1998):

- Don't judge your participants. Don't make them wrong.
- Try to conduct the interview outside the influence of managers or supervisors.
- Remind the participant that you will give them privacy if they need it for phone calls or interruptions. If the phone rings, for example, turn the tape recorder off and don't take notes.
- Keep in mind that your posture and body language can affect the participant. If you are tired and slouching or yawning, your participant may feel that you are not interested in what she has to say.
- Provide minimal encouragement. Express understanding in a neutral fashion, perhaps by nodding to show interest without biasing answers.
- Explain the limits of your ability to help the participant or give them solutions or advice during the interview. One way to leave a positive impression is to give the participants some tips when the interview is

complete. The tips should be simple, have a positive impact, and have very little risk. You don't want the participant to try something you suggested after you leave only to suffer a major data loss.

- Ask your hosts what type of clothes are appropriate when you are planning your interviews. If you are interviewing bank managers, wear a business suit. If you are interviewing students about video games, casual clothes might be preferred over business attire although you still want to be viewed as the interviewer to legitimize your role. The following key principles apply (Bailey, 1994):
  - **Legitimacy**. Dress so that you look like an interviewer.
  - **Simplicity and conservative dress**. Dress in a way that does not distract or bias the participants.
  - **Avoid wearing clothes or objects (rings, jewelry, pins) that might identify you with a particular group or organization**. For example, do not wear any pins that identify a particular political leaning.

Just How Much Discretion Should Interviewers Have?

Interviewers using the semi-structured approach can be given discretion to do the following:

- Probe the user on a question until no new information emerges (Preece, Rogers, & Sharp, 2002).
- Prompt the user to help with recall (Preece et al., 2002).
- Modify questions to fit the particular context.
- Add or delete questions (although you may have a core question set that generally should not be deleted).
- Change the order of questions posed to the participant (unlike the structured interview where interviewers generally follow a detailed script that does not allow *ad hoc* changes to the question order).
- Vary the time spent on each question.

There are no formulaic answers to how much discretion to allow, but interview organizers should consider the experience of their interviewers (more experienced interviews can have more discretion), interviewers' depth of knowledge on the topic (more depth might allow deeper probing), and the importance of consistency of the results (part of the reason for using the semi-structured method is to have the ability to make some broad comparisons). It is important to consider how much discretion your interviewers will have during the planning and training for the semi-structured interviews.

How Should You Order Questions in a Semi-Structured Interview?

Determining the best order of questions is not an easy task, and the research is quite mixed with regard to the impact of question order on participant responses. Here are some general guidelines to consider (Schuman & Presser, 1996; Dillman, 2009; Schensul, Schensul, & LeCompte, 1999):

- Arrange questions by topic, category, or domain.
- Ask the more important questions first in case you run short on time.
- Avoid difficult, threatening, or emotionally laden questions at the beginning of the interview. Generally, you should order questions from least-to-most threatening overall or within a particular domain or category.

What Is Sensitive or Threatening Varies by Setting and Culture

When you are generating questions and are thinking about how to order them, consider that the level of sensitivity or threat associated with a question can vary by setting and culture. Even something as seemingly straightforward as asking people to describe how they do their work might be viewed as threatening if those people are using unofficial short-cuts not approved by management, which is a common situation in business settings (Schensul et al., 1999).

- Order questions according to complexity with easy questions coming first and more complex ones later.
- For questions dealing with events over time, ask first about earlier events and then move to more recent events.
- Avoid asking basic demographic questions at the beginning unless they are required for screening purposes. Ask these questions at the end of the interview or provide it to the user on a questionnaire.
- Before asking questions that might be viewed as personal, remind the participant that this information is confidential, and participants won't be identified in any way on the final report.
- Have several colleagues review the order of the questions to see if the answers to a particular question might obviously bias subsequent questions.

CONCLUSIONS

The semi-structured interview is a cross between the structured interview and the unstructured interview that allows some standardization of questions and also the freedom to explore and add new questions as unexpected topics emerge. The goals of the interview will guide how much exploration is needed.

Unstructured Interviews

AlternativeNames: Flexible interview, in-depth interview, nondirective interview, open interview, open-ended interview, qualitative interview

Related Methods: Contextual inquiry, ethnographic interview, semi-structured interview, structured interview

OVERVIEW OF UNSTRUCTURED INTERVIEWS

Unstructured interviews are conversations with users and other stake-holders where there is a general topic and agenda, but no predetermined interview format or specific questions. The general goal of the unstructured interview is to gather rich, in-depth data about the users or other stakeholders' experiences without imposing restrictions on what they can express.

Unstructured Interviews Are Challenging

Unstructured interviews are challenging, even for experienced interviewers. Common pitfalls for interviewers using the unstructured interview method include the following:

- Limited planning, training, and pilot testing
- Talking too much and not listening enough to the participant. Silences are awkward, but participants sometimes need to think before answering
- Trying too hard to get answers to each general topic or questions in each interview
- Using leading questions or prompts (Dumas & Redish, 1999)
- Focusing on note-taking rather than the interview (tape-recording interviews can reduce this burden)
- Determining how much time to spend on new or unexpected topics that are not in the interview guide
- Lacking a data analysis, interpretation, and reporting plan.

In an unstructured interview, the conversation is guided by the general goals of the project, an agenda of topics to cover, and the issues that participants feel are important. Both the interviewer and participant influence the direction of unstructured interviews. Unstructured interviews require interviewers to be open to unanticipated topics, but also to be wary of conversations that ramble or participants who may get long-winded and repetitive.

"Unstructured" does not mean unprepared. Interviewers need to define the goals of the interview clearly during planning and proceed with an agenda of the main topics. The agenda may change as the interview unfolds. One of the skills of a good interviewer is to realize when the conversation reveals a new issue or a different perspective on an old issue.

The document that contains the agenda of topics or general questions is often called an "interview guide." The guide lists the areas to be covered, general questions to start a line of inquiry, and a checklist that can serve as a memory aid.

WHEN SHOULD YOU USE UNSTRUCTURED INTERVIEWS?

You can use unstructured interviews to do the following:

- Gather data on general themes rather than specific questions.
- Develop new insights about the user's interactions with technology.
- Investigate a new product and get a sense of first impressions and features that catch the eye of the user.
- Explore a new domain where you are not certain of the major issues facing users and other stakeholders.
- Gather information on sensitive or emotional topics.
- Understand how experts solve problems. Experts often possess much tacit knowledge that requires a skilled interviewer and an unstructured format.
- Follow up on a quantitative interview where some qualitative data are needed to clarify the meaning of the quantitative findings.

Unstructured interviews often last from one-half to two hours. Interviews that are too long may reduce the pool of qualified participants because they don't want to give up valuable work or leisure time. Interviews that are too short may not provide enough time to establish rapport and cover the topic in sufficient depth. Consider arranging unstructured interviews that last about an hour unless you know that the participants are dedicated and willing to give up more time (Robson, 2002, p. 273).

Unstructured interviews can be done at any time during the development cycle (Table 3.1), but they are most useful during the early stages (problem definition, requirements gathering, conceptual design, prototyping, and detailed design) when you are trying to understand general issues and determine if your perception of the issues is similar to that of your users and other stakeholders. The small bar charts in Table 3.1

Table 3.1 Method Scorecard for Unstructured Interviews

Overall Effort Required	Time for Planning and Conducting	Skill and Experience	Supplies and Equipment	Time for Data Analysis
▓▓▓▓□	▓▓▓□□	▓▓▓▓□	▓□□□□	▓▓▓▓□

Most Useful during These Phases

Problem Definition	Requirements	Conceptual Design	Detailed Design	Implementation
✓	✓	✓	✓	

provide a sense of the overall effort, planning time, skill, resources, and analysis time, required to conduct unstructured interviews.

STRENGTHS

Unstructured interviews have the following strengths:

- They provide direct experience with users and stakeholders.
- Establishing rapport with participants in unstructured interviews may be easier than it is during semi-structured and structured interviews because unstructured interviews are less formal and more conversational.
- Interviewers have more flexibility in how they word questions and probe for details than in other, more structured, styles of interviewing.
- Participants can describe issues in their own words, so unstructured interviews can be useful in understanding the users' vocabulary and any metaphors that are relevant.
- Unstructured interviews can reveal issues that the interviewer had not considered before (and may not have asked about on more structured interviews).
- Unstructured interviews sometimes provide insight into political issues that can affect product design and acceptance.
- Unstructured interviews may provide a more relaxed atmosphere than highly structured interviews where interviewers are limited in their ability to probe and explore paths important to the participant.
- Unstructured interviews can be used to gather information from key stakeholders (in addition to users) so the issues important to these stakeholders don't pop up later and derail the effort.
- Unstructured interviews can provide important insights for the design of more focused semi-structured and structured interviews and surveys. For example, you can use the results from unstructured interviews to create more complete response categories to closed-ended questions.

WEAKNESSES

Unstructured interviews have the following weaknesses:

- Becoming skilled at facilitating unstructured interviews takes time, practice, and frequent assessment by colleagues.
- Even small studies can generate large amounts of qualitative data, so the analysis and interpretation of the data can be quite

time-consuming. For example, a one-hour video recording or audio-tape from a talkative person might take anywhere from three to ten hours to review and transcribe. After the data are transcribed, the analysis of the "raw" data can take many more hours.

- Taking notes during unstructured interviews can be difficult because the participant can digress or ramble. Digital audio or video recorders are recommended, but some sites may not allow any recording. Conducting interviews in pairs (if your budget allows) can reduce this problem because one person can conduct the interview while the other person focuses on taking detailed notes. Notetakers should remain in the background and let the interviewer conduct the session so the participant isn't switching attention back and forth like a fan at a tennis match.
- Unstructured interviews have no set format, so each interview is a novel event that requires a skilled and flexible interviewer.
- The data are rich but not replicable.
- Large amounts of data may require expensive and complicated qualitative analysis software.

WHAT DO YOU NEED TO USE UNSTRUCTURED INTERVIEWS?

This section provides a brief description of the basic resources needed to conduct an unstructured interview.

Personnel, Participants, and Training

Unstructured interviews can be conducted with a single interviewer if you are using some recording equipment. If you cannot record the interview, a notetaker should accompany the interviewer. Ideally, the notetaker should have familiarity with the domain, terminology, and product to make note-taking easier and more accurate.

Unstructured interviews are perhaps the most difficult style of interview because they provide the least structure for interacting with stakeholders and require lengthy training and preparation. Novices should accompany experienced interviewers, practice, get feedback from colleagues before doing real interviews, and be involved in the development of interview guides.

Hardware and Software

Unstructured interviews can benefit from audio recorders or video recorders so you have a complete record of the interview. Digital cameras can be useful for documenting the physical environment and any artifacts that are important to the study topic. If you plan to conduct a large number of interviews, consider using a specialized qualitative data analysis tool for categorizing the qualitative data.

Documents and Materials

Documents and materials for unstructured interviews include the following:

- An interview project plan that describes the goals of the study, the recruiting plan, the background on the companies and people you are going to visit, the general topics that are of interest, the guidelines for interviewers, and the data collection and analysis plan. The level of detail depends on the magnitude of the study, but even small studies can benefit from a project plan.
- A letter of introduction that you can send or e-mail to prospective participants and their management.
- Consent forms for recording and data collection.
- NDA forms (these may not be required) if the participants have not already signed a form.
- Some type of database or software for storing and analyzing qualitative data (if you expect to have large amounts of data). You may want to examine data over a period of time or compare it to other sources of data, so some way to store it other than Post-It® Notes can be beneficial in the long run.
- Interview agendas or guides with the general areas that you will cover and potential probing questions.
- Maps and good directions.
- Small gifts or incentives for your hosts and those interviewed. See Chapter 6 for more details.

●●●————————————————————————————

Beware of Bribery

Some companies have codes of business conduct that have statements about the propriety of gifts of property or cash. Before you provide cash or gift certificates or other types of incentives, check the code of conduct at your company or organization to see if there are any issues that might get you in trouble with legal. This author has run into this several times and had to obtain permission from legal compliance groups to give away gift certificates ranging from $25 to $100.

PROCEDURES AND PRACTICAL ADVICE ON THE UNSTRUCTURED INTERVIEW METHOD

This section provides a brief description of the basic steps needed to conduct an unstructured interview.

Planning and Developing the Unstructured Interview

To plan and develop the unstructured interview, follow these steps:

1. **Determine the goals of your unstructured interviews and make sure that all your topics have a solid connection to those goals.** Examples of interview goals include the following:
   a. Understanding the social, organizational, technical, and physical environments of your users
   b. Understanding how current technology is used
   c. Understanding tasks and workflow.
2. **Recruit participants who meet your sampling criteria far in advance because interviews in the field can take from days to months to arrange.** The lead time for some interviews may be weeks, especially for very busy people. After you select your group of participants, send them an invitation that explains the following:
   a. Who is conducting the study
   b. Why they were selected
   c. The general goals and procedures for the interviews, including how long they will take
   d. The process for collecting data (recording devices, notetakers)
   e. How the data will be used and how you will keep it private.
   You might consider some contingency plans for people who cancel or forget, especially if you are traveling to their site. One important thing to do is call the participants a few days before the session.
3. **Develop an interview guide that lists the general topics or questions that you want to cover and a basic script for the interview guide.** The interview guide should have an outline of the briefing, the list of primary topics or questions, probing questions for different topics, a list of neutral prompts that interviewers can refer to (especially those who are new to unstructured interviews), and an outline of what to cover in the postinterview debriefing.
   Table 3.2 is an example of an interview guide for an experienced interviewer who wants to understand what it is like to work as an order-entry clerk for a large e-commerce corporation.

Table 3.2 Sample Interview Guide for an Unstructured Interview

Interview Guide for Order-Entry Design Project

Introduction

- Introduce yourself to participant.
- Explain the purpose and duration of the study.
- Explain privacy guidelines and how the data will be handled.
- Note what you will do if the person has to answer the phone or gets called out.
- Describe the unstructured nature of the interview, and note that you may want to cover some things in more depth than others.
- Ask if there are any questions before starting.

A Day at Work

- Describe a recent day at work.

Understanding the Work Environment

- How do you prepare for work when you arrive in the morning? Do you talk with anyone about the day's work?
- How is work assigned?
- Describe what systems, documents, and tools you use during the day.
- Describe the different types of calls that come in (e.g., new order, check on existing order, problem with an order).
- What is a typical workflow from the time that a call comes in until a call is complete?
- What types of calls do you like most/least?
- Describe several things you could do to improve your work environment.

Background on the Participant

- How did you come to this line of work? (Don't need details, just a summary. Get experience at this position and previous positions that are related.)
- How does management assess your performance? How do you know how well you are doing from day to day and month to month?
- Describe some events that were positive experiences in your job. Describe some negative experiences.

Debriefing and Final Checklist

- Follow up on any unfinished issues (e.g., you may want to collect some demographics using a short questionnaire).
- Ask if the participant has anything he or she wants to add.
- Make sure all forms are signed.
- Thank the participant, pay him/her if appropriate, and reassure him/her about privacy of the data.
- Ask if you can contact him/her briefly if you have questions about notes (only if cleared in advance with management).

Here are some practical tips for constructing an interview guide for unstructured interviews:

- The guide should be simple and free from excess clutter so the interviewer can glance at it quickly. Weiss (1994) notes that a guide is like a teleprompter for an actor or politician. You don't want to be reading it verbatim.
- The guide should be readable from a clipboard (or tablet computer) that the interviewer holds during the interview session. Experiment with text size when you are pilot testing the guide and interview procedures.

- Less-experienced interviewers may require more detailed guides to avoid moments of silence; more experienced interviewers, who are familiar with the interview topics may need only sketchy guides.
- If your guide becomes too detailed or you feel that you need to cover all the items, you may be moving in the direction of a semi-structured interview. Keep the guide for unstructured interviews general, and don't feel pressured to cover all items in every interview. Some unstructured interviews may focus on a subset of topics that are especially important, so there should be no pressure to cover every topic (although across interviews, make sure that you have reasonable coverage for all your main topics).

4. **Learn enough about the domain of interest to ask good questions and understand the general terminology used by participants.** You don't need to be an expert, but you do need to be credible.

Database Disaster: A Tale of Embarrassment and Lost Credibility

This author once set up interviews with a company interested in purchasing a complex decision-support tool. The customer was database savvy, and some of my colleagues weren't. Soon after we arrived and began the interviews, the host (a very senior manager) at the customer site called my manager and complained that my colleagues "didn't even know what a 'join' was in a database." The customers felt that we were wasting their time and were technically ignorant. The interviewers were sent home.

This event was hard on my colleagues who were experts in usability but were relatively new to database terminology and principles.

Before the next set of interviews, everyone had to take a self-administered course on database design. Subsequent interviews with database-savvy customers went much more smoothly, and we never got thrown out again because we were deficient in database principles and vocabulary!

---

5. **Develop a data collection and analysis plan that includes an outline of how you gather, analyze, interpret, and present the qualitative data you get from your interviews.** Plan sufficient time for working with data. There is no single set of conventions for analyzing qualitative data.

6. **Set up a few pilot sessions to practice your interviewing skills.** This is a cardinal rule for all user-centered design (UCD) methods. The pilot session can breed confidence, weed out poor questions, and increase the odds that the actual interviews will be productive. Even expert interviewers with decades of experience should conduct a pilot test.

7. **Create and assemble any forms or documents that you need, including the following:**
   - Screeners and letters that you use to recruit participants
   - The interview guide with an agenda, probes, prompts, and so on
   - An informed consent form if needed
   - An NDA if needed. Send the NDA to the participants beforehand; ask them to read it before the study and bring the signed copy. Have blank NDAs and consent forms on hand in case a few participants forgot to sign the documents
   - Receipts for any compensation paid to participants.
8. **If you are visiting different companies, prepare a briefing memo for each company that describes how the company uses your product, what main issues the company faces, and the agenda for the day.** Also include the name of the participants, their locations, their phone numbers, and a brief note about their role with the product of interest. An example template for a briefing memo is shown in Table 3.3.
9. **Develop a calm and confident attitude.** An interviewer must be calm, confident, credible, knowledgeable, flexible, and professional, without being arrogant. This professional attitude is set when you make first contact and reinforced as you set up interviews. Your first few minutes with the participant are likely to set the stage for the success of your interview. Robson (2002, p. 274) recommends the following rules for interviewers:
   - Listen more than you speak. Peer review during training and pilot testing can provide useful feedback on listening and prompting skills.
   - Ask questions in a straightforward, clear, and nonthreatening manner. Avoid questions that tend to blame the participant, even in subtle ways. Never put the blame on the user by saying "you didn't answer my question."
   - Eliminate cues that lead participants to respond in a particular way.
   - Be curious, interested, and engaged.
   - Enjoy the interview (or at least look as though you do). Avoid any hint of boredom or anxiety. This last rule implies that you should be careful about scheduling too many interviews in a day. Whenever possible, schedule short breaks between interviews to consolidate your notes and write down questions that you might want to pose in subsequent interviews.

Table 3.3 Outline of a Briefing Memo for a Set of Four Interviews at a Client Site			
GENERAL INFORMATION			
Title of Project:			
Company Name:			
Dates of Visit:			
Description of Company			
Company/Organization URL:			
Address and Directions (attach map to memo):			
Background Notes:			
INTERVIEW INFORMATION			
Interviewers:			
Interview Host:			
Contact Information:			
Location:			
Objectives of Interviews:			
Notes and Cautions:			
Participants Name	**Appointment Time**	**Location**	**Reminders**
Participant 1			
Participant 2			
Participant 3			
Participant 4			
Agenda		**Approximate Time**	
Meet host			
Group introductions to participants			
Overview of interviews			
Individual interviews			
Debrief with hosts			
Leave interview site			
General Observations (filled out at the end of all interviews)			
Major Issues/Unresolved Issues/Problems			

Conducting an Unstructured Interview

To conduct an unstructured interview, follow these steps:

1. **If possible, meet with all the people you plan to interview in a group at the beginning of the day, and give everyone an overview of your general plans (e.g., you will be audiotaping, the interview will take about an hour).** If you can set up this "group introduction," you can save time (you don't have to repeat material for each person),

make sure that there is a schedule for the day's interviews, start building rapport, and, if appropriate, have everyone fill out any required forms. Don't try to force the group introduction, but ask if it would be possible so everyone can get the basics all at once. This can save significant time if feasible. Of course, your recruiting and introduction letters should contain a summary of this information, but significant time can elapse between your invitation and actual visit, so you need to go over this information as a group or with each individual.

Also consider carefully your body language during interviews. Are you showing approval or disapproval with facial expressions or changes in posture?

2. **When you meet each respondent, ask him or her where you should sit.** If you need to set up any equipment, make sure that you don't interfere with anything in the participant's space. Consider whether privacy during the interview is more important than being in the participant's actual work space. If the interview is potentially sensitive, consider asking during your planning if there is a private place for the interview.

3. **Review the interview plan with each participant (briefly if you did a group introduction).** This should be outlined as part of your script. Mention the following to the participant:

   a. Some background about yourself

   b. A brief description of the interview topic and goals, the stages in the interview, recording and ethical issues, and comments about prompting and also cutting short some discussions to ensure that there is good coverage

   c. How he or she was selected

   d. Assurances that the data will be treated as confidential, and any data in reports will be anonymous. Describe what you will be doing with the data and (if you plan to send anything back to the participants) how they can get a summary of the results. If you do not plan to let the participants (or the managers who arranged the interview) see any data, be very careful what you say about the results.

   e. The amount of time that is allocated to the interview.

   f. What you will do if the person has to answer the phone or leave momentarily (e.g., shut off all recording equipment and offer to step away).

   g. The fact that there are no right or wrong answers in the interview.

h. A statement that the participant can interrupt at any time and ask questions about the topic or line of questioning.

Remember that the participant is doing you a favor, so this introduction is important for making the interview a pleasant experience.

4. **Begin the interview with some warm-up questions that are easy, non-threatening, and relevant.** It is generally important to gather some background on the participants and also to understand the context in which they are using a product or service. Avoid asking many demographic questions (e.g., education or age) at the beginning; ask them at the end of the interview. While these questions may meet the criterion of easy, they may not be directly connected to the purpose of the interview (Dillman, 2000, p. 94).

5. **During the main part of the interview, you explore the topics or questions in your interview guide and new topics that you judge relevant to your goals.** As you are conducting the interview, listen for and explore inconsistencies to clarify misunderstandings, understand conflicting beliefs, or gain new information. It is not necessary to get answers to every question at each interview. During this time, you may want to probe some topics more deeply. Hackos and Redish (1998) provide many tips on techniques for probing and "keeping the conversation going," including the following:

   a. Neutral prompts such as "uh-huh," "yes, that's interesting," and "I see what you mean."

   b. Active listening (Hackos & Redish, 1998; Tamler, 1998), where you paraphrase the participants' words in a nonjudgmental way to check your interpretations of their experience. Active listening requires a tone of voice and expression that indicates your interest in knowing more about that topic while keeping a reasonable level of neutrality.

   c. Probes for getting more details, such as "Tell me more about..." and "What happened then?" or direct questions that indicate what the interviewer really wants to know.

   d. Ways to clarify information and terminology, and validate interpretations. Hackos and Redish (1998, p. 287) note that it is important to separate what the person actually says from your interpretation of what he or she said.

6. **When you are nearing the end of the unstructured interview, consider a "cool-off" period (Robson, 2002) where you ask a few final questions that are relatively easy and do not create any anxiety.** Always

ask if there is any other information that the user would like to share before completely closing the discussion.

7. **Signal a clear end to the conversation by thanking the participant, putting away note-taking materials, and turning off any recording devices.** If you have promised any payment or other compensation for the interview, give it to the participant, have him or her sign a receipt if necessary, and ask if it is okay to contact the participant if any questions occur during the data analysis and interpretation. You should have received permission from the managers who sponsored the interviews to make future contacts.

"What Are You Writing?"

Although it has been a rare event, this author has had interviewees ask what was in my interview notes. As a general guideline, any notes taken by the interviewer or assistant should be written so you would feel comfortable if the interviewee did ask if he or she could read your notes.

After the Unstructured Interview Session

When your interview has concluded, follow these steps:

1. **Write up your notes in a summary form as soon as possible after each interview.** To make things easier, you might want all the interviewers to summarize their notes in a consistent manner. You might consider writing any notes in the interview guide as one approach that will cut down on data analysis later.

2. **Make sure that you have all your forms, tapes, and materials marked with a code for that interview so you don't waste time when you begin your data analysis trying to figure out which notes go with which participants.** If the participant gave you any artifacts, label them with a code for the interview.

3. **Write-protect any files, audiotapes, or videotapes to prevent accidental erasures.**

4. **Record any observations, ideas, questions, or reflections on the interview as soon after the interview as possible**. This is very important for unstructured interviews. You might try to give yourself fifteen minutes between interviews as well as time at the end of a day to jot down emergent questions, topics, or themes that you want to ask the next person.

VARIATIONS AND EXTENSIONS TO UNSTRUCTURED INTERVIEWS

The following section describes variations and extensions to unstructured interviews.

Informal Interviewing

Bernard (2006) describes "informal interviewing" as an interview method "characterized by a total lack of structure or control" (p. 211). His context is that of anthropology and in this context, he is referring to conversations heard in the field. In some contexts, such as internal software development, we are often engaged in hallway or office conversations about product issues. The relevant issue here is that these informal interviews should be captured in some "field notes" quickly with as much detail as possible. Hallway conversations are valuable, but all too often, we fail to jot down the essentials for later use.

Validating Lists of Responses After Several Interviews

After conducting several interviews, you may collect lists of items in response to particular topics or questions. Consider presenting the list of items to subsequent participants asking for validation, corrections, additions, or more detail. Don't start checking your lists too early so that you cut off new information. Consider gathering data from four to six participants before presenting your lists to the remaining participants.

MAJOR ISSUES IN THE USE OF THE UNSTRUCTURED INTERVIEW METHOD

The following section describes some major issues that you need to consider if you are planning unstructured interviews.

Using Probes

Probes are techniques for getting participants to provide more information or additional details without leading them so much that you only get what you want to hear. Probes are especially useful when you have participants who tend to give brief answers (in the extreme "Yes" or "No" answers to questions without elaboration). There are many types of probes (Bernard, 2006), and Table 3.4 lists some common ones.

Table 3.4 Examples of Different Types of Interview Probes

Type of Interview Probe	Example
Silent probe	The interviewer remains silent and waits for the participant to say more. This can be very difficult, especially for less-experienced interviewers.
Neutral probe	Participants are encouraged by minimalist affirmations such as the following: "Uh-hum" "Yes, I see"
Clarification probe	"What do you mean by (word or phrase)?" "So you are saying (paraphrase what the person said)?"
Give me more detail probe	"Could you tell me more about that?" "Can you give me an example of XXX?" "How did you do that?" "Why exactly did you say that?"
Emotions probe	"Can you tell me why you feel so strongly about XXX?"
Variations probe	"How has your approach changed over time?" "Do you always perform task XXX this way?"
Long question probe	This probe uses long questions to induce the participant to provide longer answers. For example, instead of a "How do you make a sale?" question, you might ask, "What are all the things that you have to consider when you are trying to sell product XXX to a new customer?"

To Record or Not to Record

A major issue with unstructured interviews is whether to record the interviews. Over the past two decades, recording and detailed reviews of audio or video have been deemphasized because of the costs in time for making and analyzing transcripts. Depending on the goals of your interview, you might use audio or video recording for the following reasons:

- Provide backup for your notes.
- Provide detail for your notes that couldn't be captured in real time.
- Make partial transcripts that highlight only major issues and extract quotes (especially useful if you didn't have a dedicated notetaker).
- Make detailed transcripts (very time-consuming).
- Provide actual comments from participants that you can include in presentation, highlight tapes, and reports.

Among the various types of interviews described in this book, the unstructured interview is the best candidate for audio or video recording because it is not quite clear how the interview will flow from session to session. Trying to take detailed notes may be difficult for the interviewer and distracting to the participant.

Taping allows the interviewer to concentrate on the flow of the conversation rather than on detailed note-taking. Weiss (1994) recommends recording because handwritten notes often leave out useful information and details of examples, and they minimize the emotional content in the responses of participants. Recording is also important if you feel that someone may question your results and want to see the raw interview data.

Practical Tips for Recording Interviews

- Consider whether the use of recording equipment deters candor. For example, if you are interviewing a physician who might worry about describing problems with medical software (and so violate privacy and risk malpractice suits), you might consider taking notes, rather than recording, or listening carefully and writing down as much as you can remember immediately after the interview.
- Make sure you have secured permissions, in writing, for recording your interviews. Bring those permissions with you to the interviews in case the security organization questions you about the recording. (This author once got several levels of permission to visit a highly secure research site. Interviews were set up and my name was on the list of approved visitors. After being escorted to a cubicle, I started to set up a video camera. A few minutes later, armed guards surrounded me, grabbed my camera, and hauled me off to a locked room. The problem was that my special video recording approval had been lost, and the chief of security was on vacation. An hour later, the security office found my form, called the chief on vacation, and the interview was restarted. Part of the approval for the recording was that the tapes would all be left with security, and my notes would be reviewed before leaving the building. Being hustled off by armed guards was somewhat disconcerting!)
- Be very clear about who gets to use the data from the recorded interviews. This author has had companies request copies of tapes "to find out what the employees are saying about the new system." This request had to be refused because it violated the rights of participants.
- Practice with your recorder before you get to the interview. Practice will help you appear professional as you set up your equipment. Fumbling with a video camera or the latest digital recorder can reduce your credibility as well as waste the participant's time.
- Take extra batteries, digital tapes, chargers, and the manuals for your recorders. Make sure everything is charged and ready for data collection. Miniature digital recorders that can store many hours of recordings on removable memory are a good investment, although if there is

a problem, you do run the risk of losing an entire day's worth of data. A conservative strategy with digital voice recorders is to download the voice file onto a laptop after each interview or at lunch.

- Take a power strip with you if you are videotaping long interviews. Spare outlets can be rare in some environments.
- If you can't secure permission to use audiotaping or videotaping, consider taking a colleague with you who can take accurate notes. As soon as an interview is over, review the notes with your colleague and fill in any gaps. If you don't have recording equipment and are working alone, consider scheduling time between sessions to add any additional comments to your notes.

Bias in Unstructured Versus Structured Interviews

There is often concern about the ease with which bias can creep into the free-flowing unstructured interview because there is no definitive set of questions, only a loose script or guide. Some might suggest that only semi-structured or structured interviews should be used because they are relatively free of biases, but the reality is that *all* types of interviews can suffer from both subtle and blatant biases. A structured interview, for example, can be strongly biased by asking leading questions such as "Describe what made the product unusable for you," or including biased response categories that force answers in a particular dimension (like those found in many political surveys). Biases can certainly be introduced into the report conclusions by interviewers who deemphasize views that don't support their beliefs.

The following are the most important ways to avoid bias:

- Be aware of the potential biases.
- Include procedures to minimize obvious biases.
- Train interviewers (and notetakers, data analysts, etc.) on how to detect and minimize biases.
- Make sure that you don't minimize results that go against your expectations.
- Periodically review interview records (tape and transcripts) to see if any biases are creeping into the interview process.
- If you plan to use multiple interviewers, consider doing some group training on interviewing techniques and working on some general consistency among the interview team.

Above all, remember that there is always some bias involved in any evaluation technique (Snyder, 2003). For example, everyone wants the products that their company is working on to do well in the market— that is a bias all interviewers need to keep in mind when interviewing current or potential customers who are interested in the best product, not necessarily your product. The best you can do is try to minimize the obvious biases and be vigilant about hidden and emergent biases.

Prepping the Participants

When you are recruiting interview participants, provide them with some background and goals of the interview. After you have recruited your participants, consider whether it would be useful to send them some very general questions (perhaps a subset of those in the interview guide) to think about so they can provide additional depth during the interview.

CONCLUSIONS

The unstructured interview is a method where detailed questions are not planned. Interviewers start with some general topics of interest and develop questions as the interview unfolds. Unstructured interviews provide rich qualitative data, but the unbounded approach to questions can make it hard to establish patterns. The unstructured interview is perhaps the most difficult of the three basic interview methods.

Phone Interviews

Alternate Names: Phone questionnaire, phone survey, telephone survey

Related Methods: Semi-structured interview, structured interview, unstructured interview

OVERVIEW OF THE PHONE INTERVIEW METHOD

Phone interviews are generally semi-structured or structured interviews conducted over the phone or through some Internet audio service such as Skype or Microsoft Lync that serves as a virtual phone. Many remotely moderated usability studies combine moderation with phone interviews.

Conducting a phone interview may, at first, appear to be a simple (and cheap) way to gather data from users and other stakeholders. Phone interviews, however, are not so simple for many reasons related to the lack of visual cues for the interviewer (Bourque & Fielder, 2003a; Dillman, 1978).

In this chapter, the main focus is on procedures and issues that are specific to phone interviews.

WHEN SHOULD YOU USE PHONE INTERVIEWS?

You can use phone interviews to do the following:

- Conduct traditional structured or semi-structured interviews with participants who are not available for face-to-face interviews.
- Support remote usability testing where you combine tools that let you see what the participant is doing with a product with questions and prompting using a phone.
- Gather data that cannot be collected through direct observation because of costs, security, or sensitivity.
- Gather usability data from international participants without the expense of travel, food, and lodging.
- Interview participants of alpha and beta versions of a product to get their initial reactions and, perhaps more importantly, their reactions after they have used the product for a period of time (Bly, 1997).
- Follow up on the results of other types of studies such as beta test sessions, usability testing, online surveys, or participant observation.
- Screen for more detailed interviews. Rogers, Gilbert, and Cabrera (1997), for example, conducted 100 phone interviews to understand usage patterns of automated teller machines (ATMs) and problems encountered with the devices by older adults. The data provided general information about usage and also served as a screener for a

smaller sample of participants who would provide more depth about their ATM experiences.

Phone interviews can be used during any phase of the product development cycle (Table 4.1). The small bar charts in Table 4.1 provide a sense of the overall effort, planning time, skill, resources, and analysis time that are required to conduct phone interviews.

STRENGTHS

Phone interviews have the following strengths:

- Phone interviewing is generally less expensive than face-to-face interviewing.
- Phone interviewing eliminates any effect due to the appearance of the interviewer (although as noted later, accents and speech patterns can affect responses and refusal rates).
- Phone interviews are useful when you have participants or stakeholders in widely distributed geographical areas.
- Phone interviews can have a shorter data collection period than face-to-face interviews. For example, you could interview fifty people in a week by phone; the same number of face-to-face interviews might take several weeks or longer.
- Phone interviews may have a better response rate than mail surveys (Bourque & Fielder, 2003b; Fowler, 1993), especially if you have a connection with the participants (e.g., they are users of your product).
- Phone interviews can be used in combination with prototype evaluations (Ratner, 2003) and other UCD methods such as field visits and online surveys.

WEAKNESSES

Phone interviews have the following weaknesses:

- Phone interviews can be quite taxing, so they are generally shorter than face-to-face interviews. Phone interviews longer than twenty to thirty minutes probably require dedicated participants who are strongly invested in the outcome of the interview or interviewers with a very good "phone personality" who can keep people on the line (Bernard, 2006, p. 263).

Table 4.1 Method Scorecard for Phone Interviews

Overall Effort Required	Time for Planning and Conducting	Skill and Experience	Supplies and Equipment	Time for Data Analysis
▢▢	▨▨▢▢	▨▨▨▢	▨▢▢▢	▨▨▨▢▢

Most Useful during These Phases

✓	✓	✓	✓	✓
Problem Definition	Requirements	Conceptual Design	Detailed Design	Implementation

- Phone interview questionnaires are more complex to develop than self-administered questionnaires because the phone version must include a script for the interviewer as well as the questions, response categories, and prompts and procedures for clarifying ambiguous, mumbled, or incomplete answers. For example, if you ask a person to rate something on a scale from 1 (extremely bad) to 5 (extremely good) and that person says "Pretty good," how do you ask them what that means on the 1 to 5 scale?
- Structured phone interviews with many rating scales and conditional questions ("If the answer to Question 3 is option A, then go to Question 9") can be taxing (and demotivating) to both interviewers and participants.
- Participants have to remember the questions and response categories, so questions (and possible responses) cannot be too complex.
- Phone interviews are not as good as face-to-face interviews when you are dealing with complex issues (Shuy, 2001).
- UCD practitioners with pronounced accents or speech impediments may not be good interviewers over the phone.
- If you have multiple interviewers, you have to worry about consistent approaches to the interviews and group training, which increases the cost of the phone interview.
- Phone interviews are often conducted at times that are convenient to the participant but not for the interviewer (evenings, early mornings, weekends).
- You don't know what is going on in the participant's setting while you are asking questions. Imagine getting a call for a phone interview around 11:30 A.M. when you are working at home and in the middle of preparing a quick hamburger for lunch. It is difficult to answer questions for a structured interview while flipping a hamburger with one hand and holding the phone with the other.
- The structure of the phone questionnaire is very important because a participant who misses a single word may find a question nonsensical but be too embarrassed to ask the interviewer to reread the question.
- Interviewers and participants may get fatigued by questions that are repetitive. For example, consider how fatiguing it is to answer ten rating-scale questions where the interviewer is required to read all the options of a 5-point scale *every* time (Strongly Disagree, Disagree, Neither Disagree Nor Agree, Agree, Strongly Agree) and then ask the participant to choose an answer.

WHAT DO YOU NEED TO USE THIS METHOD?

This section provides a brief description of the basic resources needed to conduct a phone interview.

Personnel, Participants, and Training

The phone interview method may seem simple, but it requires several types of training. The interviewers must be trained to establish rapport and keep that rapport throughout the interview. Developing rapport in a few minutes is a skill that requires training, practice, and adaptability. Following are several specific ways to develop rapport with a participant:

- Minimize the status or power difference between the interviewer and participant. Shuy (2002) found that an interviewer could promote equality by using conversational language (e.g., contractions and saying "uh-huh") rather than the formal language of highly structured interviews.
- Avoid the use of "I" when speaking to the participants ("I want you to rate the following items …").
- Sound energetic and enthusiastic.
- Do not jump into the questions right away.

The phone interviewer should conduct the interview at a pace that matches the participant's level of comfort. This can involve quickly assessing and matching the participant's speaking speed (Robson, 2002). Part of the training for telephone interviewing can involve dealing with participants who speak slowly and those who speak so quickly that it is hard to capture their answers. Consider training and pilot testing that involves some extremes of verbal style.

Interviewers must be sensitive to the cognitive demands of the questions and be prepared to prompt the participant without biasing the results. Interviewers must keep the participant focused on the interview questions and know when to close out responses to one question and move on to the next.

Here is a suggested outline of a training program for telephone surveys using multiple interviewers. This outline is for larger studies, but it can be adapted for small groups of UCD practitioners:

1. Interviewers complete a self-study or formal course on general interviewing skills and specific skills related to telephone surveys.

2. Interviewers are introduced to any hardware or software that will be used for the survey and practice using the tools to administer the survey.

3. Interviewers conduct mock interviews on the phone. The interviews are critiqued by an experienced interviewer or by other members of the UCD team.

4. All interviewers go over the specific telephone survey question by question (and response by response). Best practices are covered for handling various situations (refusals, sensitive questions, prompts, scheduling of callbacks, what to do if a participant changes his or her answer after a response has been recorded).

5. A small set of pilot interviews are conducted with target participants. A debriefing is held at the end of the pilot interviews.

6. Issues that arise during the pilot interviews are discussed, and any procedures that emerge from the pilot interviews are written up and distributed to all interviewers.

7. Periodic debriefings are held with all interviewers during the remainder of the phone interviews to discuss any problems or issues.

Hardware and Software

The hardware and software for telephone interviews can vary in complexity. At one extreme, no special hardware and software support for the actual interview is provided other than creating the printed documents described in the next section. At the other extreme are highly automated interviewer workstations where specialized software autodials from a list and presents the interviewer with the introductory script and an electronic questionnaire where the participants' answers can be entered directly. On a smaller scale, interviewers can develop online telephone surveys using survey software or database software such as Microsoft Access. The surveys include instructions and prompts, branching, skipping, and some basic data analysis.

Documents and Materials

The following primary documents and materials are used for phone interviews:

- An interview plan.
- A recruiting screener.

- An introduction letter or message that explains the phone survey process. This isn't possible if you are doing random digit dialing (RDD) but is recommended if you know the names, e-mails, or addresses of your participants.
- A paper or computerized questionnaire for the interviewers.
- A questionnaire that is modified for the participants that you send out beforehand to make the phone interview easier. (This is recommended as a way to reduce the cognitive load. Consider asking participants to make notes on the questionnaire to prepare for the phone interview.)
- A call log to record calls and the outcome of the calls.

PROCEDURES AND PRACTICAL ADVICE ON PHONE INTERVIEWS

This section describes the basic approach for conducting a small- to medium-scale phone interview study using from one to five interviewers. The assumption here is that you will not be hiring a company to do the phone interviews for you.

Planning a Phone Interview

Follow these steps to plan a phone interview:

1. **Decide if a phone interview is the appropriate method for your research goals.** Examine your goals against the strengths and weaknesses of the phone interview methods that are listed earlier in this chapter.
2. **Develop a phone interview plan that describes the following:**
   a. The business and user experience goals for this study.
   b. The general questions that you want to ask (they should all be related to the business and user experience goals). At this point in the plan, you are not looking for the exact wording of the questions.
   c. The user profile and recruiting plan. The recruiting plan, whether done in-house or by a professional recruiter, should include the following:
      - The sampling method (many times, it will be a convenience sample, but you might also want to do a more sophisticated sampling of your users or customers), the sampling frame (the set of participants that has a chance to be selected, given

the sample method that has been chosen), and sample requirements. See Chapter 6 for more details on sampling methods.
- A recruiting script that explains the study. The language of
the recruiting script must be tailored to your audience.
- Any incentives that you plan to offer the participants.
d. The process for developing and testing the phone interview
procedures.
e. The process for collecting, organizing, analyzing, and interpreting the data (e.g., you might want to include multiple coders
for qualitative data and procedures and requirements for inter-
rater reliability).

Know the Law Before Recording Phone Interviews

In the United States, there are both state and federal laws regarding the
recording of phone conversations. You need to check with a lawyer on
the details for your project.

State laws in the United States vary with regard to recording phone
conversations. A majority of states require one-party consent, but some
states require that all parties know that a conversation is being recorded
(all-party consent). If you are conducting a group phone interview with
people in many different areas (who are not part of your company or
organization), it is important that everyone know that the conversation is
being recorded (so if someone comes in late to a "phone focus group"
for example, you should inform that person that the call is being
recorded).

If you are calling people in different parts of the country (in effect,
crossing state borders), the law is fuzzy. For example, if you live in
Maryland, where there is all-party consent, and interview a person who
lives in Washington, DC, where there is one-person consent, which law
takes precedence? Play it safe if at all possible and go by the more restric-
tive law.

The law for recording calls within a business (e.g., you are recording
interviews with internal stakeholders) are somewhat different. US federal
law has a "business exception" that deals with the recording of employee
phone conversations.

International laws dealing with the recording of phone conversations
vary as well. With the increase in remote testing of international customers, it is worthwhile to check with someone in the target countries
about recording phone calls.

Check with your lawyer if you plan to record phone calls to determine what type of written, verbal, and audio notification and opt-out
procedures are required.

3. **Consider how the phone interview is different from face-to-face interviews, e-mail surveys, paper surveys, or web surveys, which are methods that UCD practitioners may have more experience with.** The basic differences are listed here (Dillman, 1978):

   a. The questionnaires for phone interviews are designed for the interviewer, not the participant. Questionnaires can contain notes, prompts, and cues for navigation between questions. Dillman (1978, p. 200) cautions that "...excellent mail questionnaires do not make very good phone questionnaires." The colleague who thinks that he or she can grab a mail or online questionnaire and convert it easily to a phone questionnaire is making a mistake (Bourque & Fielder, 2003a).

   b. The cues that are present in face-to-face interviews are generally absent in phone interviews. This makes it more difficult to establish rapport and credibility with participants.

   c. Questions are read to participants, so there is a chance for interviewer bias to creep in to the phone interview. There are software tools that can "read" questions to participants and accept spoken or telephone keypad input, but the total lack of human contact may result in a lack of credibility.

   d. Few UCD practitioners have had formal training or experience in phone interviewing methods. Although much time is spent in UCD programs on face-to-face interviewing for laboratory and field projects, little time is generally spent on the details of phone interviews.

   e. Participants in phone interviews may tire of repeated similar questions, so interviewers need to keep enthusiasm high while avoiding substantive bias.

   f. Response categories ("not at all satisfied," "somewhat satisfied," etc.) for verbal questions can be hard to remember and must be repeated often, if not every time a question is asked.

   g. Questions must be worded carefully so they read well and sound good to the participant.

4. **Construct a draft phone questionnaire.** Consider the following principles for designing questionnaires that are appropriate for phone

interviewers (Bourque & Fielder, 2003a; Dillman, 1978; Lavrakas, 1993):

a. Consider making questions short but not so short that you are compromising the goals of the interview.

b. Make your questions specific and precise. This might require you to ask multiple short questions to get at the levels of specificity and precision that are required for your research goals.

c. Avoid too many response categories. In an online or paper survey, you might use a 7-point scale. For a phone interview, you might use a 5-point scale to minimize the memory requirements.

d. Consider creating a version of the questionnaire for your participants and sending it to them before the phone interview so they have the questions and response categories in front of them. The problem with this approach is that the questionnaire for the respondent and for the interviewer can be quite different (e.g., the interviewer questionnaire has instructions, prompts, and notes that the participant questionnaire does not).

e. Design the interviewer questionnaire so that it is easy to read and follow, especially when the interviewer is the only one recording the answers. Make it easy to record answers (e.g., you might make it easier to circle answers than write them in; if you are typing notes on the keyboard, design the online form for easy navigation and response selection). Don't split questions across pages. If you have answers where you need to skip to different pages, make it clear where to go.

f. Put clear instructions and hints on the phone interview questionnaire about how to handle common questions or problems.

5. **Choose interviewers who are easy to listen to for the length of your phone interview.**

6. **Begin recruiting your participants early.** Recruiting is a complex topic, and there are many ways to recruit participants. You could pay a recruiting firm to find participants, recruit participants from

Table 4.2 Phone Survey Letter Template
May 10, 2013
Participant Name
Title
Organization
Address
Dear [insert salutation and name]
The User Experience Team from [company/organization name] is conducting a study about your experience with [insert product name]. We want to understand how you use our product, what works well, and what aspects of the product we can make more useful and usable for you. We are specifically interested in [list some of the key issues that you are investigating]. Your name was chosen from our Customer Council list because of your background and experience.
In the next week or two, an interviewer from our team at [insert company and organization name] will be calling to schedule a phone interview with you. If you are willing to be interviewed, the interviewer will schedule time for a 30-minute session that will be convenient for you. With your permission, we would like to record the interview so we capture all your feedback accurately. Your participation in this study is purely voluntary. If you agree to speak with us, you can withdraw your participation at any point before or during the interview.
The interview will cover the following topics:
• [Topic 1] • [Topic 2] • [Topic 3] • [Topic 4] • [Topic 5]
All the information that we collect is confidential, and no names or organizations will be reported in any reports, publications, or presentations. Only members of our User Experience Team will have access to the data. If you have any questions about our study or do not want to be contacted, please send an e-mail or call [insert name/title/organization] at [insert e-mail and phone number].
Your input to our study will be used as input to future product requirements and design improvements. We hope that you will have time to help us with our study.
Thanks for your consideration and helping us make our product more useful and efficient.
Sincerely,
[Name]
[Title]
[Organization]
[Contact information]

internal databases, or use viral marketing through online user or customer forums. One useful tool for recruiting is an advance letter that describes your study and explains why a person might want to participate. Table 4.2 is an example of an advance letter template that you can modify for transmission by mail, fax, or e-mail.

7. **Train your interviewers.** Training topics should include:
   a. **How to operate the phone.** This seems obvious, but with complicated digital and Internet phones, you should, for example, know how to put someone on hold and how to turn off your ringer so it doesn't disrupt an interview (if you have multiple numbers). If you are using a headphone rather than a speaker phone (the sound quality is better), you should practice plugging the headphone in, adjusting the volume, and adjusting the microphone for the best quality.
   b. **How to answer questions that participants have about the interview study.** Dillman (1978) suggests creating a list of common questions and standard answers. This answer sheet is also important for providing consistent answers to common questions if you have multiple interviewers. Your answer sheet, in addition to answering general questions, might have notes on the individual questions that you ask during the interview.

Common Questions Participants Ask During Phone Interviewers

   1. How did I get chosen for this interview?
   2. How do I know that this is authentic?
   3. I have colleagues you might like to interview, could you interview them?
   4. How long will this take?
   5. How will I be paid?
   6. What are you going to do with the data?
   7. Can I reschedule this call?
   8. If we get interrupted, can I call you back?
   9. Who is sponsoring this phone interview? Can I talk with him or her?
   10. Will my data be anonymous/confidential?

---

8. **If possible, conduct a few face-to-face pretest interviews with target participants to better understand their issues.** You can use these interviews to refine your phone script and get a sense of some of the issues that might come up over the phone.
9. **Pretest the interview "on the phone".** Conduct interviews over the phone to get comfortable with prompting, filling in answers, and navigating around the paper or online form. You might start with

a practice phone interview with colleagues to refine the procedure and then test several people in the target audience.

10. **Revise the phone questionnaire and your procedures.** Create a "rule book" or interview specification (Bourque & Fielder, 2003a; Dillman, 1978) that does the following:

a. Provides a checklist for what to do before, during, and after an interview.

b. Describes how to get hold of the correct person for the interview (e.g., leave message on an alternate phone number, page the person, send an e-mail).

c. Describes the rules for conducting the interview. For example, the interviewer might be asked to read questions exactly as they are written.

d. Describes what to do if a person does not understand a question. For example, you could reread the question.

e. Describes how to probe when there is ambiguity or a misunderstanding.

f. Explains what verbalizations from the participant actually count as answers. For example, if a participant says "uhm, ahah," does that count as a "Yes"?

g. Describes what to do in awkward situations (the person whispers that his boss is nearby, and he can't tell you everything he wants to tell you; the person has a work emergency; the person thinks you are technical support).

h. Describes what to do when the interview is complete. For example, you need to note the time, go over every answer, make sure your notes are legible (if you took handwritten notes) and will make sense in a week. Make sure that any data forms or online data sheets are coded properly.

Conducting the Phone Interview

To conduct the phone interview, follow these steps:

1. **Send an e-mail, send a letter, or call a few days or weeks ahead to remind people of the phone interview.** If they need to have anything ready for the interview, include that in your reminder.

2. **If you get ahold of a person and he or she will not be available at the designated time, have a schedule of other available times at your fingertips.** Include times early in the morning, in the evening, and even on weekends (unless the goals of your study dictate that it is critical for the person to be in his or her office). If you are interested

in web sites that are used mostly at home, you may want evening hours, for example.

3. **Establish rapport and use a conversational and pleasant tone of voice.** If you get tired, take a break, or better yet, schedule breaks into your interviewing days.

4. **Pace your interview to cover the necessary questions.** Make sure you get to the most important questions first. Avoid extending the interview beyond the time you established with the participant.

5. **Keep a detailed log of your calls.** Include whether you conducted the interview, the reasons for any interviews that didn't occur, the time that you began and ended the interview, and any follow-up that you might need to do (e.g., a good customer asks you to send some information).

After the Phone Interview Session

After the interview, follow these steps:

1. **Review your notes at the end of the interview.** If issues came up that you might want to ask subsequent participants, make a list of those issues or questions and make sure that all the interviewers have this list with priorities for subsequent interviews.

2. **Keep a record of any suggestions for improving the interview process.**

3. **Take an adequate break between interviews.** Make sure that your schedule does not cause burnout.

VARIATIONS AND EXTENSIONS TO THE PHONE INTERVIEW METHOD

The next section describes variations and extensions to the phone interview method.

The Phone Usability Method

Ratner (2003) describes a discount usability method she calls *phone usability*. In a phone usability scenario, a think-aloud phone interview is conducted while the participant works on several tasks with a prototype or working web site (Ratner's focus is on the web although this can be done with software applications or even hardware products). Phone usability entails the following steps:

1. **Write a usability test plan for the phone usability study that describes the business goals and tasks that reflect those goals.** The test plan should include pretask questions, the tasks themselves, and standard

debriefing questions. The rationale behind each question and task should be described.

2. **Make a prototype or the current site or product available to participants.** Ratner notes that prototypes can come in many forms (HTML, paper, working versions, Microsoft PowerPoint slides) but recommends that the prototypes look more like sketches so participants will feel like their input has a chance to be considered. Several different methods of making prototypes available are useful because the participants may not have the appropriate software (e.g., Microsoft PowerPoint) or may not be allowed to accept attachments inside their companies (a fax machine may be a backup).

3. **Recruit the participants in a variety of ways.** Generate a recruiting script and/or message for recruiting. Consider small incentives. Schedule sessions for about thirty minutes.

4. **Confirm the dates, times, and requirements for the testing with the participant.** Make sure that you describe the goals of the study and how the data will be used. Ratner notes that in every communication with potential participants, it is important to stress that the product is being evaluated, not the participant.

5. **Conduct practice and a pilot session for the facilitator and notetakers.** Prepare a "best practices" handout for the observers.

6. **Conduct the phone interview.** Because the phone interview is often shorter (thirty minutes versus one to two hours) than a typical laboratory usability test, only a few tasks can be covered. If there is time, observers can pass questions to the facilitator who will pose them to the participants.

7. **Conduct a debriefing at the end of each phone interview.**

8. **Conduct a final debriefing, analyze the data (including comments about the method), and prepare a report.**

Ratner did some return on investment (ROI) calculations comparing a typical phone usability test with a traditional usability test (each with five participants) and found that the phone usability test could be conducted at about one-third the time (two days versus one week) and one-third the budget ($2150 versus $6775). One trade-off that is discussed by Ratner but not included in the ROI calculation is the more limited amount of data (and number of tasks) that can be dealt with in a phone usability session. Ratner has a detailed list of advantages and

Table 4.3 Advantages and Disadvantages of the Phone Usability Method	
Advantages of the Phone Usability Method	**Disadvantages of the Phone Usability Method**
Rapid feedback on rough prototypes can be collected quickly.	There is generally no visual image of the user working with the prototype.
This method can complement other discount and nondiscount usability evaluation methods.	Distractions can mar a phone usability session.
No special equipment is required.	Speaker phones can disturb people who are adjacent to the participant (in business settings especially). Headphones work better, but there is still an issue of the person thinking aloud and disturbing those around him or her. An important part of recruiting for any type of phone interview or phone usability session is to arrange a time and place where the participant will not be disturbing others (this should be stated on the recruiting messages and confirmation). Some people may decide to have you do the interview in the evening when they are home (after dinner, and the children are in bed).
The ROI of phone usability is high.	Observers may not be as involved as they would be actually watching participants work with a product or prototype.

disadvantages regarding the phone usability method; several of the more important ones are given in Table 4.3.

MAJOR ISSUES IN THE USE OF THE PHONE INTERVIEW METHOD

The next section of this chapter describes some major issues that you need to consider if you are planning phone interviews.

Technology and Cultural Influences on Phone Interviews

The use of answering machines, cell phones (with no national directory in 2013), no-call lists, use of e-mail as a phone replacement, and caller ID have cut response rates for phone surveys and made it more difficult to know who is included and excluded from surveys.

Callbacks

Telephone surveys, much like mail surveys, must consider the number of attempts that should be made before a particular number is abandoned. If you are doing a small survey of known participants (e.g., beta customers who volunteered to provide feedback), this may not be a major problem, but if you are using random digit dialing (RDD) or another method where you have no strong connection with the potential participants, your interview plan should deal with the issue of callbacks. Shuy (2001) notes that callbacks can backfire and lead to a higher refusal rate and, in those cases where callbacks do result in interviews, inferior data from the callbacks who agree to participate. Groves and Kahn (1979) recommend that the first few minutes of a telephone interview be dedicated to developing verbal rapport and not data gathering.

A decision that investigators must make regarding callbacks is whether a message should be left and what the specific message should be. If messages are left, they should generally be short, polite, and consistent across the participants (Lavrakas, 1993).

Length of Questions

Long or complex questions can be difficult for participants in phone interviews. One solution is to keep all questions short and simple. However, the objectives in some phone interviews may require questions that don't fit the short and simple principle. Dillman (1978) suggests that complex questions include some redundancy in the form of a key word summary. The redundancy makes complex questions even longer but helps the participant mentally organize the main points of the question before answering. The summary comes just before the response categories are read to the participant.

Too Many Response Categories/Long Response Categories

In a paper or online questionnaire, you can include long lists of responses for questions. For example, your questionnaire might list ten job titles (plus "Other") or 7-, 9-, or 10-point rating scales with text labels such as the following:

+3	Extremely Good
+2	Quite Good
+1	Slightly Good
0	Equally Good and Bad
−1	Slightly Bad
−2	Quite Bad
−3	Extremely Bad

+2	Extremely Good
+1	Somewhat Good
0	Equally Good and Bad
−1	Somewhat Bad
−2	Extremely Bad

The 7-point scale on the left is appropriate in a paper or online questionnaire. The 5-point scale on the right is easier for participants to remember during a telephone interview. When developing your phone questionnaire, limit the number of response categories.

Long response categories can also be a problem for your participants. When you conduct your pilot testing over the phone, note whether people ask you to repeat particular response categories.

The Order of Questions

When you are developing a phone questionnaire, the order of questions is important for engaging the participants and reducing resistance to the interview, creating a conversational flow, easing the memory and cognitive burdens for participants, and improving the overall quality of the data. The general rules of ordering are similar to those for questionnaires:

- Make the first questions especially relevant and interesting so you can capture the person's attention and interest in your research. Few people will drop out of phone interviews once they answer the first few questions. Good initial questions serve as a foot-in-the-door (Goldstein, Martin, & Cialdini, 2008) that will lead the participant to finish the rest of the phone interview.
- The first question should generally be relevant to everyone in the study. Later questions can be relevant to particular subgroups.
- Lay out your questions in a logical order that progresses from easy to hard. Avoid sensitive questions early in the phone interview. After the participant has answered some of the early questions, he or she will be more open to providing sensitive information because the interviewer has established some rapport. Make the first question interesting and nonthreatening (e.g., don't ask about salary, a common question on those phone survey calls you get at dinner time).

- Put all demographic questions (except those needed for screening) at the end; you want to start with questions that are relevant to the participant, and questions about age, job title, and company name are not really relevant to the respondent (although they might be critical to the interviewer). Putting demographic questions at the beginning of questionnaires is one of the most common errors in survey design.
- Group questions by topic. Consider clear transitions when you move from one topic to another. Within a topic, group questions by format. For example, ask all your rating questions together followed by other question formats (open-ended, ranking, etc.).
- Put objectionable questions near the end of the questionnaire. Keep in mind that income, employment status, and age are often sensitive topics. If you are doing phone interviews during work hours, consider that your participants may not want personal information or income to be overheard by their colleagues.

The Order of Responses

On telephone surveys, there is sometimes concern that the order in which the responses to closed-ended questions are read could bias the results (a primacy effect where the first answer is remembered or a recency effect where the last answer tends to be remembered). The solution to this is to randomize or rotate the answers where this makes sense (it wouldn't make sense for rating scales but might make sense when there is no true ordering to the response options). Computerized telephone surveys can be designed to automatically change the order of responses for each interview. If paper-and-pencil methods are used, the order of responses could be changed by having different forms for each interview or having an algorithm for the interviewer to read the responses from a different starting point for each interview (this last method may be prone to error).

CONCLUSIONS

The phone (or Internet audio) interview method may seem somewhat dated, but in the world of global products, phone interviews can be an effective method for gathering data. While phone interviews seem simple, there are many best practices that can enhance the interview process and produce useful and rich data for product designers.

CHAPTER 5

Focus Groups

Alternate Names: Focus group interview, focused interview, group interview

Related Methods: Focus troupes, questionnaires, semi-structured interview, structured interview

OVERVIEW OF FOCUS GROUPS

A focus group is a qualitative research method where a moderator (sometimes called a facilitator) guides a group of five to twelve participants through a series of questions or exercises related to a particular topic in a nonthreatening environment (Krueger & Casey, 2000; Morgan, 1997). Focus groups are group interviews where topics supplied by the moderator are discussed among the participants with the moderator controlling the time spent on particular topics.

The participants in a focus group are chosen because they have been (or could be) involved with a particular product, service, or situation, or because they share characteristics relevant to the topic at hand (Langford & McDonagh, 2003). For example, people who are looking for jobs using various Internet services might be asked to give their opinions about features, content, or branding in a new job site.

Focus groups are generally held away from the participants' home or work sites and last from one to three hours. A focus group study is rarely based on a single event; usually, there is a series of three or more sessions to determine if there are any common and divergent patterns or themes. Depending on the goals of a focus group, the researchers might hold sessions in different geographical locations or recruit participants from different sized companies to ensure that the findings have some generality.

There are several types of focus group—each focusing on somewhat different goals (Kuniavsky, 2003):

- **Exploratory focus groups** are used when the goal is to elicit and understand general attitudes toward or perceptions of a product or service. You might ask people, for example, to describe their experience with online grocery shopping. The results from exploratory focus groups can be used as input to surveys or other methods.

- **Feature prioritization focus groups** are used when you want to examine what features appeal to your users and customers. O'Donnell, Scobie, and Baxter (1991) used this type of focus group to get opinions about specific features of a home heating control system and used feedback from focus groups to redesign the user interface. You can have people rank features using methods such as the q-sort or the monetary method and discuss the results. Wilson (2008), for example, used the monetary method where you ask people to "buy a set of requirements on a fixed budget" at a user conference to determine which new features a company should focus on during the next development cycle.
- **Competitive analysis focus groups** are used when you want to understand what value people see in competitive products or even different approaches to a particular design.
- **Trend explanation focus groups** are used when you try to understand what is driving a trend in user or consumer behavior.

Focus groups have a history going back more than eighty years (Kuniavsky, 2003; Merton, Fiske, & Kendall, 1956; Morgan, 1997; Robson, 2002), and there is considerable literature and research on focus group methods, often from a marketing perspective. However, in the realm of UCD, there is much debate about the appropriate use of focus groups and the validity and reliability of focus group data (Kidd & Parshall, 2000; Langford & McDonagh, 2003; Nielsen, 1997). While focus groups are not replacements for the direct observation of users, usability testing, and other forms of user research and evaluation (Hackos & Redish, 1998), they are quite useful for understanding people's attitudes, perceptions, and values (Kuniavsky, 2003; Langford & McDonagh, 2003). Focus groups in UCD can incorporate activities, such as questionnaires, brainstorming, observation of product use, creative exercises, mini-user trials, and collaborative prototyping that can mitigate some of the criticism leveled at traditional focus groups (Bruseberg & McDonagh, 2003).

WHEN SHOULD YOU USE FOCUS GROUPS?

Focus groups are useful for eliciting the following:

- A range of ideas or reactions to a particular topic.
- Attitudes, preferences, and opinions on a topic.

- Information that could be helpful in designing other studies. For example, you might use a focus group to understand something about terminology and motivation.
- Information to help you understand confusing results from a quantitative study that you have already conducted.
- Reactions to product concepts.
- Feedback on competitors.
- General problems with a product or service.
- Descriptions of events that last over a period of time.
- Issues with current products or work environments (Kuniavsky, 2003).
- Questions that you might want to ask in a subsequent survey (Bernard, 2006).

Focus groups are most useful during problem definition, requirements gathering, conceptual design and implementation (Table 5.1). The small bar charts in Table 5.1 provide a sense of the overall effort, planning time, skill, resources, and analysis time, required to conduct focus groups. They can also be used during implementation to get feedback on working products and services.

STRENGTHS

Focus groups have the following strengths:

- The focus group method is relatively inexpensive (compared to many individual interviews) and can be arranged quickly.
- Focus groups produce concentrated amounts of data in a short time.
- Focus groups used early in a project can produce insights and questions from the interaction among different users or customers of products or services. This type of synergy might not occur with individual interviews, surveys, or other methods.
- Focus groups can provide a flexible approach for data collection (Langford & McDonagh, 2003). There are not strict procedures for running focus groups. Focus groups can include many activities, including mini-usage studies, surveys, and prioritization of items. The procedures described in this chapter and other references are guidelines—not mandates. You can modify focus group questions on the fly, ask people to give opinions privately before

Table 5.1 Method Scorecard for Focus Groups

Overall Effort Required	Time for Planning and Conducting	Skill and Experience	Supplies and Equipment	Time for Data Analysis

Most Useful During These Phases

Problem Definition	Requirements	Conceptual Design	Detailed Design	Implementation
✓	✓	✓		✓

group discussion, and investigate new topics that emerge during the session.

- Focus groups are useful for getting feedback on how people work over a long period of time (Nielsen, 1997). In a sidebar to Nielsen's column on focus groups, Meghan Ede describes how she gets data on the activities that are part of the participants' typical day or week—something that other methods may not capture at all.

WEAKNESSES

Focus groups have the following weaknesses:

- The conclusions that you can draw from a focus group are limited because the sample may not be representative of the larger population. Most focus groups are comprised of samples that do not permit the extrapolation of any quantitative data such as frequencies or percentages.
- Dominant individuals can skew the results of a focus group. An excellent moderator can use various techniques to reduce the influence of a dominant individual, but this is still a common weakness of the focus group method. Khan (2003) tells a story about a focus group where a single participant was insistent about using a drop-down list for navigation. Soon, the entire group was agreeing with the "drop-down list guy," and the client who was observing said "let's do a drop-down." A prototype with a drop-down list for navigation was tested and the result—"drop-downs annoyed users."
- Conflicts and power struggles can arise between participants with strong personalities.
- Focus groups are often conducted by outside consultants who may not have the domain experience to probe deeply (although questions can be fed to the moderator during a session).
- Moderators need considerable expertise to deal with a wide range of group dynamics.
- Focus groups are not a good method for gathering data on detailed work activities.
- The data from focus groups can be difficult to transcribe if multiple people try to talk at the same time. A good moderator will have only one person talking at a time to make transcription or notetaking easier.

WHAT DO YOU NEED TO USE FOCUS GROUPS?

This section provides a brief description of the basic resources needed to conduct focus groups.

Personnel, Participants, and Training

The skills required to become a good focus group moderator require considerable practice and assessment. UCD practitioners who work alone should consider doing some focus group sessions with internal colleagues that do not entail significant risks to credibility and build up to external sessions. A colleague, preferably one skilled in conducting focus groups, should observe and take notes on the new moderator's interaction with participants and provide feedback on the strengths and weaknesses of the interaction. Robson (2002) stresses the need for pilot or even pre-pilot sessions with explicit moderator assessment and training before focus groups.

Focus group moderators usually follow a printed or online discussion guide with a set of questions, topics, and exercises. The discussion guide can be based on questions that emerged from other data sources such as brainstorming, surveys, observations of users, or individual interviews.

The skill of the moderator is a key to a successful focus group. Skilled moderators must do the following (Krueger & Casey, 2000; Stewart, Shamdasani, & Rook, 2007):

- Balance empathy and sensitivity against objectivity and involvement.
- Believe that all the participants in a focus group study have some wisdom they can share (and keep that belief after running multiple sessions).
- Involve all the participants.
- Not speak too much or give away their particular feelings or attitudes about the topics of the session.
- Generate interest in the discussion topics and keep the focus group energized.
- Be reasonably consistent in the way he or she asks questions within a particular session and between sessions.
- Ensure that the participants are answering the target questions and not skirting the question or going off on a tangent.

- Know enough about the topic to put answers in context and understand the comments of participants.
- Keep dominant personalities from monopolizing the session or going off-track.
- Know when to follow a line of inquiry that isn't part of the discussion guide. Unanticipated responses can often lead to valuable insights.
- Know when a line of inquiry is not likely to lead to useful data.
- Avoid giving away the expectations of the sponsors.
- Analyze the data and extract themes and main points from the session.
- Present a written and oral report of the themes and other findings.

Hardware and Software

Traditional focus group sessions are generally recorded using digital audio or video systems. If you are doing international focus groups, you may want your translator to record the translation onto a separate audio track. If you use a focus group to get feedback on a prototype, an existing product, or brand images, you may want to use a facility or portable lab that allows you to include the image you are projecting with a video of the focus group participants so you have a clear connection between what the participants are seeing and their comments about the prototype or product.

Documents and Materials

The important documents that you need for a focus group include the following:

- Screening tool for recruiters.
- Confirmation letter with instructions on how to get to the focus group site and contact information.
- Rescreening questionnaire. The rescreening questionnaire is a document that the focus group facility administers to each participant when he or she arrives to ensure that the person is qualified to participate. This form should use some of the same questions that were on the original screening tool with the possibility of an "articulation question" to determine if the participant will be effective. Articulation questions are generally open-ended questions that can show how well people can communicate (Greenbaum, 1993). Participants who fail at this articulation question are paid and excused.

- Consent form (which might include an NDA).
- Moderator's guide.
- Receipts for payment of incentives.
- Questionnaires and exercises for participants.

Other materials for focus groups may include projection systems for displaying information, flip charts, markers, tapes, sticky notes, and masking tape for attaching large sheets of paper to the walls (e.g., the results of brainstorming).

PROCEDURES AND PRACTICAL ADVICE ON FOCUS GROUPS

This section describes the how to conduct face-to-face focus groups.

Choosing a Moderator

The choice of a moderator is perhaps the most important choice you can make in your focus group planning. Consider the following criteria when choosing a moderator from inside or outside your organization (Blankenship, Breen, & Dutka, 1998; Kuniavsky, 2003; Greenbaum, 1993):

- **Level of experience of the moderator.** Consider how many focus groups the person has done in the past year and how long the person has been conducting focus groups.
- **Professional moderators versus in-house moderators.** Professional moderators can be found in most urban areas. Professional moderators have experience handling the complex dynamics of focus groups but may not have much domain or product experience for your particular product. In-house moderators may have the domain and product experience necessary to probe and ask good questions, but they can also be aware of product history and politics and may struggle to remain neutral. Professional moderators can cost several thousand dollars a day (or per session), plus the cost to develop the moderator's guide, analyze the data, and present the results.
- **A good memory for names and the participant's words.** The dynamics of a group are much more positive with a moderator who can remember names and doesn't call someone by the wrong name. Large name cards (sometimes called "tent cards") that are clearly visible from the furthest point in the focus group room can be an important memory aid. In addition to remembering names, the

moderator should be able to use the words of the participants when rephrasing what they said to further the discussion.

- **Similarity between the moderator and the participants.** Barrett and Herriotts (2003) reported on focus groups with older participants and suggested that having a moderator who was close in age to the participants was important for putting them at ease.
- **Sufficient domain knowledge to understand the issues, vocabulary, and context of questions and comments.** This is more important for highly technical discussions. An excellent general-purpose moderator may work well for consumer sites, but that same moderator may struggle if the focus group deals with network performance monitoring or 3D visualization issues for an architectural design tool. At a minimum, the moderator should have reasonable knowledge of the concepts and terminology and enough general background on the topic to probe and follow up on questions and comments. There is a trade-off here between using internal colleagues and hiring an outside consultant. While it might cost you a bit more money, it is worthwhile building in enough time to brief and prepare external consultants if they are not specialists in your particular domain area.
- **Credibility with the stakeholders and sponsors of the focus group.** Would you pay attention to results from a moderator that you did not find credible?
- **The ability to listen carefully to the participants and to formulate questions quickly that tap issues not in the interview guide.** While the questions in the discussion guide are the primary areas of interest, focus groups can often veer into unexpected areas that are as important as the original set of questions. The ability to pick out important new (unanticipated) ideas that emerge from the group and press for more comments, explanation, and details is a critical skill for moderators.
- **The ability to deal with strong personalities and to refocus the group when the discussion wanders from the topics of interest.** A good moderator must be able to switch quickly from a free discussion on one topic to a discussion on a new topic without seeming too dominant. One strategy that a moderator can use is to stress in the introduction and ground rules that he or she will sometimes have to cut off discussion to cover key issues.
- **A neutral approach when asking questions and encouraging discussion (Kuniavsky, 2003).** Moderators should be careful about expressing their views about the topic of the focus group. Moderators must

even be aware of nonverbal behaviors such as nodding that might indicate endorsement of a participant's statement. If the rest of the participants believe that the moderator has a particular stand on a question or topic, that might stifle conversation. This is an issue for moderators who, like many of us, play roles in the design of the products or services under discussion.
- **Genuine interest in the topic of the focus group.** A bored moderator who doesn't seem to care about the topic can yield poor results.

Planning a Focus Group Session
Follow these steps to plan a focus group session:

1. **Decide how many groups and how many participants per group are needed to support your goals.** The criteria for recruiting participants depends on the goals of the focus group, but there are several general criteria (Bernard, 2006; Blankenship et al., 1998; Kuniavsky, 2003):
   a. **Multiple locations.** Do you need to conduct focus groups at different locations because of known or suspected regional differences? You may, for example, want to run studies in different regions of your country to see if different themes or patterns emerge.
   b. **Group size and homogeneity.** The literature on focus groups generally recommends that the size of a group should be six to twelve participants (Bernard, 2006). If the topics are sensitive, then you might want the group to be smaller, say four to six participants (Morgan, 1997). Krueger and Casey (2000) also recommend small focus groups of six to eight participants because the small groups are easier to control, and participants have more time to express themselves. If you have a large group, you might get people whispering to each other because they don't get enough speaking time. When deciding the size of the focus group, consider whether you want broad information (larger groups) or more in-depth information (smaller groups).
   Merton, Fiske, and Kendall (1990, p. 137) summarize the guidelines for the size of the group:

   The size of the group should manifestly be governed by two considerations. It should not be so large as to be unwieldy or to preclude adequate participation by most members nor should it be so small that it fails to provide substantially greater coverage than that of an interview with one individual.

Just as important as the size is the homogeneity of the group. In focus groups, too much diversity can dampen discussion, so consider what demographic and domain characteristics are important (e.g., experience, education, age, profession, seniority) and aim for reasonable homogeneity.

How Many Groups Should You Have?

The rule of thumb from marketing and social science (Morgan, 1997, p. 43) is that a focus group study should consist of three to five individual focus groups; the theory here is that conducting more sessions yields diminishing returns. The actual number of groups in your study will depend on several factors (Greenbaum, 1993; Stewart et al., 2007):

- The complexity of your topic and the number of distinct groups that are being considered.
- The variability of your participants within and between sessions. The more variability you have, the more participants you need to see coherent patterns and themes emerge.
- The degree of structure in your focus groups. Here structure refers to the degree of standardization that you choose for your interview questions. More structure means fewer groups. The degree of structure depends on whether you are exploring new territory or have a fixed agenda.
- Your budget (this is the primary gating factor).
- Your deadlines for results.
- The geographic distribution of your participants. Are they coming from different suburbs, or are they more focused in the downtown area near your site?

Don't Forget to Over-Recruit!

You will often lose a few people for focus groups because they have work or family emergencies, get caught in traffic, or meet the man or woman of their dreams and decide a date will be more fun than a focus group. Consider over-recruiting by about 20% (Morgan, 1997). If you have planned on a ten-person focus group, you might recruit twelve people who can be squeezed into the session if they all show up. Barrett and Kirk (2000) recommended that planners of focus groups involving older participants over-recruit by 25%. If you have participants who are doctors or lawyers with schedules that are often determined by factors outside their control, consider over-recruiting as well.

c. **Familiarity of participants.** During recruiting, consider the impact of familiarity on the dynamics of the group. If possible, you should avoid recruiting people who know each other. People who are friends, colleagues, or acquaintances can change the dynamic of the focus group through their own informal communication channels, for example, winks and nods (Kuniavsky, 2003). While ideally, you might want to avoid familiarity, there are times when you will be working with teams or organizations where people will know something about one another. Morgan (1997) notes that the key issue here is whether a particular group can engage comfortably in a discussion that may have some sensitivities or political consequences. If you are working inside an organization, you might, for example, attempt to minimize status differences among participants. This author once facilitated a focus group where, by chance (and a limitation of the recruiter's database), a manager and one of his employees showed up at the same focus group session. The subordinate deferred to the manager and barely spoke at all.

d. **Expertise in the focus group topic.** Participants should have enough knowledge and background about the topic of interest to provide meaningful feedback. However, you should avoid having a single guru in the focus group because that person is likely to disrupt the flow of the session and intimidate the rest of the group into deference or submission. For example, you might not want to invite a senior software engineer who works on web pages to provide feedback on your prototype home page. Stewart et al. (2007) warn that "self-appointed" experts, people who are not truly experts but who like to have others believe they are experts, often are more difficult than actual experts. There is often no clear technique for filtering out self-appointed experts, so the moderator must control these participants.

e. **Focus group experience.** Avoid "professional" focus group participants. Professional participants are people who have been in many focus groups or who enjoy the food and money more than the dialogue. Make your exclusionary criteria explicit for your recruiter (e.g., "Participants who have been in more than two focus groups in the past year are not acceptable.")

2. **Prepare a screening questionnaire that has both the inclusionary and exclusionary criteria.** If you have an outside recruiter, be very clear

about the exclusionary criteria. For example, you might want to avoid the following:

a. People who have been in previous studies sponsored by your organization.
b. Participants from direct competitors.
c. Journalists or bloggers who might reveal what you are doing (even if they have signed NDAs).
d. People outside a particular age range.
e. People from your own company (assuming that you are doing an external study).

3. **Prepare a moderator discussion guide that has an outline of the sequence of topics, questions, prompts, documents, and exercises.** This guide should be a joint work product of the moderator and sponsor with input and review by key stakeholders. The guide should have a schedule of how much time will be allotted to each main topic, question, or exercise, as well as any aids or materials required. A well-written moderator guide generally has the following sections (Greenbaum, 1993; Kuniavsky, 2003):

a. **Introductions.** This section covers the procedures for introducing the moderator and any assistants, the ground rules for the group, the use of recording equipment and observers, informed consent, nondisclosure requirements, and introductions of the participants.

b. **Warm-up.** The warm-up section of the moderator guide lists general questions related to the topic. If you were conducting a focus group on buying over the Internet, you would ask basic questions about buying behaviors. You would also identify probes for the warm-up questions.

c. **Detailed topics.** This section has the main questions or points that you want to cover. The various resources on focus groups suggest four to eight main questions. If there are exercises for participants, the instructions are included (you could also have an exercise in the warm-up section).

d. **Summary.** The summary section describes how you will end the session. During the summary phase, the moderator can ask if there are any final comments or advice that they want to pass on to the clients. The moderator may want to summarize the main points that came up during the session and take some time to thank the participants for their work.

Table 5.2 is a generic template for a discussion guide for a moderator based on an example from Bruseberg and McDonagh (2003).

4. **Decide if you want participants to do some homework before they arrive or engage in activities during the session that require preparation.** A common and valid complaint about focus groups is that they do not represent the work context. You won't be able to reproduce the context of work, but you can ask participants to do some limited "homework" before they arrive (Coughlin & Sklar, 2003). For example, you can ask participants to bring in some examples of their work or send them a cheap disposable camera and ask them to take pictures of their office or printouts of software that they use. If people can't take pictures or make screenshots, you can ask them to keep a short diary to record what they do or to answer questions related to the focus group topic. Coughlin and Sklar (2003, p. 133) asked participants to keep a driving diary for the three days before their focus group that described their trips with any vehicle, who was involved, what they were doing, whether the vehicle met their needs, and if they had any emotional reactions during their trips.

   Another useful thing you can do to make the session more realistic is to ask participants to engage in activities during the session that remind them of the experience in the real world. A final suggestion is to give the participants a follow-up assignment after the focus group (e.g., you might give them a demo copy of a product that is on the market but that they haven't tried yet).

5. **Conduct a pilot test of the moderator guide with a small sample of participants.** Walk through exercises to get a sense of how much time is appropriate. Modify the guide based on your pilot results. Kuniavsky (2003) suggests that you consider the first focus group as a "dress rehearsal" and allow some time to make changes after your first focus group. Given that budgets for research can be tight, dress rehearsals, however useful, may be difficult to justify.

6. **Prepare a data analysis plan that describes how the data will be analyzed, interpreted, and presented.** The analysis can range from a raw transcript that the sponsor analyzes to a summary of common themes that are supported by quotes. If quantitative data are collected during a session (e.g., prioritization exercises or product ratings), the techniques for analyzing that data should be described. If

Table 5.2 A Generic Template for a Moderator's Guide

Moderator's Guide for [Name of study]

Date: April 20, 2013	Moderator: Chauncey Wilson			
	Focus Group Number: 1			
Topic	**Description**	**Materials/Aids**	**Duration**	**Time**
Room preparation	Check and prepare the room used for the focus group; test all equipment; ensure that food and drink are ready.	Checklist for focus group	1 hour before session	6:00
Presession snacks and drinks; meet participants	Meet participants and get to know them a bit.	List of participant names	10 minutes	7:00
Introduction of the study and logistics	Describe the goal of the study; introduce yourself; note where facilities are; explain video recording/audio recording; sign informed consent and nondisclosure.	Consent forms Nondisclosure	10 minutes	7:10
Warm-up discussion	[List warm-up exercise and questions here.]		5 minutes	7:15
Topic 1	[List questions for Topic 1.]		10 minutes	7:25
Topic 2	[List questions for Topic 2.]		10 minutes	7:35
Exercise 1	[Describe Exercise 1—for example, you might have participants list words associated with a product that is described or shown to them.]	Exercise handouts or forms; or actual examples of the product	15 minutes	7:50
Feedback discussion on Exercise 1	Put your discussion question here, for example, "Please share your views on the product you read about (used) in Exercise 1."		10 minutes	8:00
Break			10 minutes	8:10
Topic 3	[List questions for Topic 3.]		10 minutes	8:20
Topic 4	[List questions for Topic 4.]		15 minutes	8:35
Exercise 2	[Describe Exercise 2—for example, you might have participants list words associated with a product that is described or shown to them.]	Exercise handouts or forms; or actual examples of the product	10 minutes	8:45
Feedback discussion on Exercise 2	Put your discussion question here, for example, "Please share your views on the product you read about (used) in Exercise 1."		15 minutes	9:00
Topic 5	[List questions for Topic 5.]		15 minutes	9:15
Discussion summary	Summarize issues and ask for any final thoughts.		10 minutes	9:25
End of session	Hand out incentives, get receipts, and thank participants.	Incentives Receipts	10 minutes	9:35

you are hiring a third party to conduct your focus groups, ask for a sample report.

7. **Decide on the appropriate incentive for the session.** The type and size of the incentive depends on the sensitivity of the topic, the length of the session, the intrinsic motivation of the participants, and the background of the participants. See Chapter 6 for more details.

8. **Prepare a set of name cards (large tent cards are recommended) with only the first names of participants.** Have some spare name cards in case of a late substitution by a recruiter. Make sure the names can be seen easily from any point in the room. You might have the tent cards prepared ahead of time so they are clearly legible. If someone prefers a nickname (or even a pseudonym), you can write it on a new card and remove the original card.

Choosing a Facility and Arranging the Seating

Follow these steps to choose a facility and arrange seating for a focus group:

1. **Choose a facility and room that is comfortable and free from distractions.** Don't seat people near windows or doors where they might be distracted by the sounds or events going on outside. The focus group room should allow you to arrange the seats in a circular or semicircular fashion. The layout of the seating can have a major impact on the interaction between the participants and moderator (Merton, Fiske, & Kendall, 1990; Morgan, 1998). Some questions to ask about the facility and the specific focus group rooms are listed here:

   a. Is it easy to find the facility? Are there maps that you can send to the participants or that they can refer to online?

   b. Is there easy parking and a clear path for the participants to follow?

   c. Are there any security issues that participants need to know about?

   d. Does the facility have tables that allow for everyone to be recorded on video?

   e. Is there room for observers? Are there any guidelines about how observers use the facilities (e.g., they might come into the observation room through a different door)?

   f. Are the facilities comfortable for two- to three-hour sessions?

   g. Are the facilities glum and dreary or upbeat and pleasant?

    h. Is the focus group and observation room soundproof?

    i. Will the facility provide computers, projection screens, easels and paper pads, pens, tent cards or nametags, and other material? If something is needed after normal hours, is there a contact on-site for the moderator to call?

    j. Is there support for any problems that might occur during a session (e.g., hardware or software malfunctions, the light switch doesn't work).

    k. Is there a copier nearby if a participant wants a copy of any consent or nondisclosure forms?

2. **Arrange time before the focus group to get familiar with the room and any equipment that is used for recording the session.** Many commercial facilities provide a technician to operate the equipment (at a cost, of course). Ask about general support and support for any emergencies.

Conducting a Focus Group Session

Follow these steps to conduct a focus group session:

1. **Do a sound and/or video test before the participants arrive to ensure that the equipment is working.** In the event that there is a hardware failure, make sure that you have a contact who can troubleshoot the system if you are not familiar with the equipment. You might consider using a high-quality digital audio recorder as a backup if you have any uncertainty about the recording equipment.

2. **Brief your observers on how to behave during the focus group.** Invite observers to the facility about an hour before the session begins so there is time to explain any rules for observing the session. The briefing includes tips on listening, staying open-minded, communicating with the moderator during the session, and interacting with the participants. Usually there is little direct interaction between participants and observers, but there are times when the observers are right next to the focus group room, so it is worthwhile to remind the observers about the rules for opening doors, meeting participants coming in or out, and speaking quietly as many facilities are not completely soundproof. Consider creating a simple form with the rules for observing and hand this form out as the observers arrive.

Active Versus Passive Observers

You can ask your observers to take general notes or even assign observers to take notes on feedback from specific participants (e.g., "Please take notes on anything that participants 4 and 5 say"). Another active observer activity is to have the observers list the three to five themes, patterns, or questions that emerged from each focus group session.

---

3. **As participants arrive, invite them to the room for the focus group.** It is useful to have some snacks and beverages like water, coffee, and tea, especially if the groups are held at night. You might want to offer food snacks only at the beginning and end of the focus group session because people who are munching can create problems for your recording. One mistake a moderator can make is to have potato chips or other crunchy food, as a snack during a session. The crunching can be so loud, especially if the cruncher is near a microphone, that the comments might be rendered unintelligible. You might want to allow drinks and "soft" food (including something vegetarian and vegan), but no crunchy foods (potato chips, celery, etc.) during the focus group interviews.

4. **Try to spend time with the participants as they arrive to get some idea of their personalities and verbal styles.** Krueger (1998) recommends that you have tent cards prepared, but that you don't place them on the table until after you assess the participants' verbal styles. The more verbally dominant people should be placed near the moderator where he or she can easily break eye contact; the quieter people should be placed across from the moderator so eye contact can be made easily.

5. **If you are using a room with recording equipment and one-way mirrors (or plan on having taping equipment as a backup), explain this to the participants, and ask them to read and sign an informed consent form.** You may also need a nondisclosure to protect proprietary information, but that can often be built into the consent form.

6. **Describe the purpose of the session, why the sponsor wants feedback, and how the data from the sessions will be used.** Focus groups often limit the amount of information about the sponsor so feelings about the sponsor do not interfere with the discussion. Some moderators are allowed to reveal the sponsor at the end of focus group

with the goal of getting additional information about customer or user feelings toward the sponsor. In some cases, such as focus groups at user conferences, the participants all know who the corporate sponsor is, but you may not want to identify the specific people involved in using the data.

7. **Create trust by emphasizing the confidentiality of the data and the value of all opinions, whether positive or negative.**

8. **Describe the ground rules for the session (from the moderator's guide).** Common ground rules include these:
   a. Only one person should speak at a time.
   b. The moderator may cut some discussions off if they go on too long.
   c. Everyone's input is important. This is an important ground rule so people who get cut off don't feel offended.
   d. For some questions, the moderator might go around the table and get input from everyone (but avoid doing this too much). If you notice that people are not engaged, try to figure out why they are quiet and what you can do to get them to talk.

9. **Have the participants introduce themselves briefly by first names only.** Be sensitive to privacy issues here. You might ask them for some brief background related to the topic of the focus group or some personal but nonintimate introductory information.

10. **Begin a session with a good general-purpose question to get people talking.** The main purpose of the first question is not to gather substantive data but to get people talking. The initial question should be easy and quick to answer and broad enough that most of the participants can answer it. Opening questions are generally not going to be important in the overall analysis. Krueger and Casey (2000) recommend that the initial question does not make any power differences among the participants salient. For example, you would not ask people, "What is your job title?" because that could reveal hierarchies that might interfere later. You might ask for the participant's name, and then your first question might be something such as "How long have you used [product or service X]?"

11. **Ask a question that introduces the topic, questions, or main issue under investigation.** This "introductory" question is often open-ended and gives the moderator some idea about the views of participants (Krueger & Casey, 2000). For example, you might ask "How did you learn about [product or service X]." Morgan (1997)

suggested that the moderator ask the introductory question and then give the participants a few minutes to write down some answers or ideas. The act of writing down some points for the introductory question puts the participants "on record" and reduces groupthink—the tendency to adapt the positions of other, more forceful people.

12. **Use a funnel approach for questions that follow the introductory question.** There are a number of approaches for conducting a group interview. A useful approach is to start with general questions and then move toward more specific questions. This is called the funnel approach and is common in both individual and group interviews (Stewart et al., 2007).

13. **Use probes to extract additional information from participants.** There are many types of probes, both nonverbal and verbal. Here are some probing techniques that you might try:

    a. Simple statements such as "Could you tell me more about that?" "Could you give me an example of what you mean?" and "Could you tell me what you mean by that?"

    b. Short pauses by the moderator. These pauses are intended to evoke additional comments from the group. Novice moderators have trouble using the five-second pause because they are not comfortable with silence.

    c. Activities such as conceptual mapping where you ask people to write down all of the items that they can think of and then group those items they feel are similar.

    d. If you are getting similar comments from the group, you might ask "Does anyone see things differently?" Avoid asking if people agree or disagree because that could engender hostility.

14. **At the end of the focus group session, the moderator should provide a summary of some of the key points that emerged and thank the participants for help.** The moderator might reiterate how the data will be used so participants feel like they have done something worthwhile.

After a Focus Group Session

Follow these steps after the focus group session:

1. **Debrief the moderator and any observers after each group session.** The debriefing should identify issues that affect the analysis

(e.g., you had a power struggle between several participants or a person who was domineering). Conduct a mini-assessment of the session on what went well and what went poorly during the session. Note any new issues that emerged for consideration in a subsequent focus group. Identify major themes or big issues that emerged.

2. **Code any data forms, videotapes or audiotapes, and notes from the session.**

From Oral Language to Written Language—The Rules Are Different

If you do many interviews, there is a good chance that you will need to hire a transcription service. You might think that transcription is a fairly mechanical process—listen and type—but that isn't quite true. The transcriber or notetaker must make decisions such as the following:

- Where do punctuation marks go?
- Do I include repetition and filler sounds/words?
- Do I make things grammatically better?
- How much do I guess when something is barely audible?
- Do I include notes about a person's nervous laughter?

Different notetakers with similar backgrounds and instructions are very likely to create quite different transcripts. Kvale (1996) and Bernard (2006) discuss practical and theoretical issues with the transcription process and offer some suggestions:

- Provide your transcription service or person with specific written instructions about transcription procedures (e.g., do you want them to include the "Hms" and "Uhhs" or note the length of pauses which may indeed have meaning) and the purpose of the study.
- If you have more than one person transcribing, have multiple people review the same recording and do a reliability check.
- Transcription can be time-consuming, especially if you do it yourself, so plan your time accordingly. Transcribing digital audio- or video recordings can take three to six hours for each hour of the interview (the time depends on the talkativeness of the participant and interviewer).
- Consider purchasing a real transcription device where you can control moving forward and backward easily using a foot pedal. Alternately, consider voice recognition software such as Dragon Naturally Speaking™. With practice, you can get the recognition level high enough to cut transcription time down considerably.

3. **Summarize your data.** Immediately after a focus group session, the moderator should walk through the guide and review the trends, questions, and comments for each topic (Kuniavsky, 2003). A notetaker should capture the discussion and note where there is agreement or disagreement. After each focus group session, identify the "big ideas" that emerged. When all the sessions have been completed, pull out the big ideas from all the sessions. There should be little controversy on the big ideas.

Do a quick edit of questionnaires, verbal responses, and other data forms soon after a session to look for moderator or participant errors. Consult the recorded video or audio if the notes are unclear and review questionnaires for obvious inconsistencies.

A basic step in the analysis of focus group sessions is to translate or code the data into a form that is countable. There are two major types of codes: quantitative and qualitative. Quantitative codes can come from closed questions or exercise data. After coding, questionnaire and other data can be tabulated into summary tables showing frequencies, percentages, and other descriptive statistics.

Qualitative data come from open-ended questions and the dialogue between moderator and participants. Setting up codes and categories for open-ended and verbal data begins with the transcription of all of the open-ended and verbal data. As data are transcribed, the analysis team (often the moderator) categorizes responses into trends, issues, and topics. Some common categories in UCD include the following:

- Mental models
- Metaphors
- Likes and dislikes
- Stories and quotations
- Problems and issues
- Differences between competitive products
- Differences between different groups or subgroups (Kuniavsky, 2003).

4. **Set expectations with your client about when reports from a single session or set of focus group sessions will be ready for presentation.**

VARIATIONS AND EXTENSIONS TO FOCUS GROUPS

The next section describes useful variations and extensions to the focus group method.

Task-Based Focus Groups

For gathering usability data, consider task-based focus groups tasks where the participants actually use products and then provide feedback. Rosenbaum, Cockton, Coyne, Muller, and Rauch (2002) suggested that usability focus groups, one type of task-based focus groups, be conducted in three phases:

1. The first phase is a group discussion where participants are introduced and presented with the topic and procedures.
2. After this group discussion, the participants can work on tasks individually or break into small groups and work on a set of tasks related to the topic. If you are interested in getting feedback on requirements, you can, for example, ask members of the group to choose the top-five requirements. You can also ask people to review a web site or work on some tasks with a prototype and provide individual or small group feedback.
3. The third phase of a usability focus group is to have the entire group discuss their feedback from the tasks. Because the participants have already produced some written or recorded feedback, they are less likely to be swayed by the opinions of dominant members.

Combining Usability Testing with Focus Groups

If you have a focus group site that is close to a computerized classroom, you can combine usability testing or walkthroughs with focus groups. Bentley College and Michigan State University, for example, have computerized training rooms where focus group participants can work on designated tasks with software prototypes or products as individuals or small groups and then move to a focus group room for a general discussion based on actual product experience.

Group Testing

Most usability testing is done with one or two participants (co-participation). Group testing (Nokia, 2004) combines focus groups and usability testing to take advantage of the strengths of both methods. Group testing is most appropriate when there is a software prototype, current version of a product, or a small set of competitive products. Participants are given a set of tasks and asked to work in small groups. The participants can be asked to take notes as they work, or a notetaker can be assigned to each of the groups. After the groups work on the tasks, a moderator walks through the tasks getting input from the groups. In addition, marketing questions such as how much would the groups pay for this product can be discussed. UCD practitioners who try group testing for the first time should consider whether the groups using a product can overhear each other and possibly influence each other or provide clues on how to complete tasks. You can reduce the chances of being influenced by others by separating the groups with portable partitions and using small portable white-noise generators to mask the conversations of groups using the same room.

Usability Round Tables

Usability round tables (Butler, 1996) bring together a targeted set of users who bring samples of their work to a site where members of the development can observe the users and ask questions about how they use the product. The usability round table is designed to be a meeting place—not a testing place. The users are recruited to discuss a particular area of interest to the developers (e.g., you might want users to describe how they create and use charts or how they choose items from an e-commerce site). During a round table, a moderator asks the users to talk about their work and work environment and then walk through applications using data sets and artifacts that they brought to the round table. The moderator and design team generate a set of questions that they want answered, but there is freedom to go beyond the standard questions. A usability round table could involve three to eight users. At the end of the round table sessions, the development team is asked if they need to see more users or want to go to a new research topic. Butler (1996, p. 28) reports that this method is useful for gathering information about the following:

- Typical size and layouts of data files.
- What features are actually used (in your products or a competitor's products).
- What features fail.
- What features users have constructed for themselves.
- How applications are built.
- How a user actually learns an application.
- How often an application is used.
- How the application is used.

Focus Troupes

Focus troupes (Salvador & Howells, 1998) combine elements of theater with group feedback about product concepts. In a focus troupe, short dramatic scenarios showing how a product might be used are presented to an audience of stakeholders, sometimes using professional actors. The stakeholders might be primary users, secondary users, or the design team itself. During the dramatic enactments of product scenarios, the "audience" engages the focus troupe in a dialogue (much like the moderator does with participants in a focus group). The dialogue can involve questions and clarifications about the product and scenario, positive feedback about the product, and comments about problems that might occur. The main advantage of the focus troupe approach is that it provides the audience with more context about a product and how it will be used than traditional focus groups. Another advantage is that the use of theatrical techniques (acting out scenarios and using early prototypes as props) is motivating and involving for participants. Details of the focus troupe method can be found in Salvador and Howells (1998), Sato and Salvador (1999), and Howard, Carroll, Murphy, and Peck (2002).

Online Focus Groups

Online focus groups are useful for getting to participants who are geographically dispersed and can reduce travel costs. There are a variety of online focus group technologies including the following:

- **Telephone focus groups.** In a telephone focus group, participants are invited to join in a group telephone discussion on a specific date and time. Participants get confirmation letters or e-mails. The participants are called the day of the focus group as a reminder. Each person is welcomed as he or she joins. If clients are remote, they can send e-mails or even fax questions that they want the moderator to ask the phone participants. Telephone interviews require very experienced moderators.
- **Web applications.** A moderator can communicate with both clients and participants using chat areas and whiteboards for presenting information.
- **Chat lines.** Hass (2004), for example, used a chat application to conduct focus groups with hearing-disabled users. Chat logs provided the data for a qualitative analysis.
- **Bulletin boards and blogs.** Threaded bulletin boards or blogs are a possible method for collecting opinions, attitudes, perceptions, and even experiences if a prototype was made available.
- **Online focus group services.** These services use proprietary web technologies that conduct focus groups for clients.

Mann and Stewart (2000) discuss some of the general issues with Internet interviewing and online focus groups. Key issues include the following:

- **Interpretations of pauses.** Pauses during an online chat can be intended by the moderator as a clue that he or she is "listening" to the participant. However, the pause might be perceived as inattention or distraction. The same pause in face-to-face focus groups might be viewed as an "attentive pause" that allows people to comment on the current topic. The lack of face-to-face contact can change the meaning of pauses.
- **Establishing rapport.** You can start to establish rapport before the online focus group by posting a welcome message that will set the tone for the session. You might ask online participants to introduce themselves and provide a description of their current surroundings or a brief note about their experience with the topic of interest.
- **Ground rules for participation.** Ground rules are perhaps more important for online focus groups than face-to-face focus groups because you don't have visual or spoken ways to retain control over the session; however, too much emphasis on ground rules can set a negative tone for participants and inhibit conversations.

Unfocus Groups to Broaden Your Perspective

In focus groups, you generally try to get a set of representative users together to discuss a product or service. In contrast, the unfocus group, a technique pioneered by the design firm IDEO, involves recruiting people who are not necessarily representative users or consumers. The online version of *Fast Company* magazine (Pink, 2003) provides an example of a carmaker who wanted to create a car that appeals to people over age 65. To understand the concerns of prospective elderly customers, some IDEO personnel conducted an unfocus group that included healthy seniors, seniors who had health problems, seniors who were car buffs, a driving teacher, and a state trooper. The goal of this type of study is to understand atypical views of a current or future product or service. You can find another extreme example of an unfocus group in a story by storyteller Steve Denning (2004). Denning tells about an unfocus group that was assembled to explore multiple perspectives toward sandals. The members of that unfocus group included an artist, a bodybuilder, a podiatrist, and a shoe fetishist—not necessarily your typical sandal wearers!

MAJOR ISSUES IN FOCUS GROUPS

The next section of this chapter describes some major issues that you need to consider if you are planning focus groups.

International Considerations

If you are planning to conduct international focus groups, consider the following issues (Honold, 1999):

- Allow time for significant planning and an understanding of local cultures. Honold (1999) gives an example of focus groups held in Germany and India that followed different approaches because of cultural differences.
- Consider employing a moderation team rather than a single moderator. Good international moderators may not possess the domain knowledge necessary for a high-quality focus group, so a moderating team with a domain or language expert in the room may be appropriate.
- Conduct focus groups in participants' native language.
- Hire professional translators. Brief translators on the goals and questions before the focus group, and then debrief those translators after each session. If you are videotaping, you can have the translation recorded on a separate audio track.

Should the Participants in Focus Groups Be Homogeneous or Heterogeneous?

Focus groups often focus on homogeneous audiences. Homogeneous doesn't mean identical, but it does mean that the participants should be similar in ways that are important to the questions and issues that you plan to discuss. Kuniavsky (2003) provides a good discussion about differences among participants that can affect the results of the focus group. For example, you might want to avoid gurus or experts (unless you want all gurus or experts for your particular problem) because they can easily dominate the entire focus group. Similarly, you might want to restrict the age range if you are investigating music (for someone in his fifties, Simon and Garfunkel might still be relevant, whereas teens may not even know about Simon and Garfunkel). Members of a focus group must feel comfortable enough with each other to talk about their feelings, attitudes, and perceptions so you need to consider if there are demographics that you don't want to mix. If there are several important subgroups (e.g., union leaders and managers), you probably want to conduct separate focus groups and then look for common themes or divergent feedback.

Anonymity and Honesty in Focus Groups

One complaint with focus groups is that the participants may not be honest in front of other people. Peer pressure can bias the results of focus groups. Kiley (2005) describes how America Online, Inc. (AOL) found that reactions to e-mail spam that emerged from face-to-face focus groups were quite different from that obtained from e-mails about spam. The conclusion was that men were afraid to admit that they didn't know how to use spam blockers effectively. Online focus groups and instant message panels where participants can view prototypes or share reactions to products or services anonymously may encourage honesty and openness.

CONCLUSIONS

Focus groups are not too popular among UCD practitioners and have been the focus of debate at international conferences. Focus groups required experienced facilitators who can control groups, think on their feet, and understand a domain well enough to choose reasonable lines of inquiry. This chapter describes how hybrid focus groups that combine traditional group interviews with exercises like polls, quick design reviews, and short usability tests can enhance the usefulness of the data and reduce some of the negative impact of groupthink.

CHAPTER 6

General Interviewing Issues

There are some common issues across different interview methods. To avoid redundancy in individual chapters, these common issues are covered in this chapter. These issues focus on sampling methods and the use of incentives for interview methods.

SAMPLING METHODS

Sampling, the process of choosing the subset of people who will represent your population of users, is a complex topic that is described only briefly here. The two major types of sampling are probability and nonprobability (Bailey, 1994; Levy & Lemeshow, 1999; Robson, 2002). In probability sampling, the probability of selection of each participant is known. In nonprobability sampling, the interviewer does not know the probability that a person will be chosen from the population. Probability sampling is expensive and time-consuming and may not even be possible because there is no complete list of everyone in a population. For many interview studies, you are likely to be dealing with nonprobability samples where you can use one or a combination of the following approaches (Bailey, 1994; Robson, 2002):

- **Quota sampling.** You try to obtain participants in relative proportion to their presence in the population. You might, for example, try to get participants in proportion to a distribution of age ranges.
- **Dimensional sampling.** You try to include participants who fit the critical dimensions of your study (time spent as an architect or engineer, time using a particular product, experience with a set of software tools).
- **Convenience sampling.** You choose anyone who meets some basic screening criteria. Many samples in UCD are convenience samples that can be biased in subtle ways. For example, the easiest people to

find might be users from favorite companies that are generally evangelists of your product. You might end up with a "positivity bias" if you use participants from your favorite companies.

- **Purposive sampling.** You choose people by interest, qualifications, or typicality (they fit a general profile of the types of participants who would be typical users of a product). Samples that meet the specific goals of the study are sought out. For example, if you are trying to understand how experts in a particular field work on complex projects, you might seek out the "best of the best" and use them for your interviews.

- **Snowball sampling.** You identify one good participant (based on your user profile or persona) who is then asked to name other potential participants, and so on. Snowball sample is useful when there is some difficulty in identifying members of a population. For example, if you are looking for cosmologists who use complex visualization tools, you might find one and then ask him or her about any friends or colleagues in the field who might want to be interviewed.

- **Extreme samples.** You want people who are nontraditional or who have some exceptional knowledge that will provide an extreme or out-of-the-box perspective.

●●●——————————————————————————————————

Extreme Input Can Be Useful

The use of "extremes" in user research can provide inspiration (Jansen et al., 2013) and help you understand the limits of a system. In addition to extreme samples of users, you can also explore extreme data sets that are large and dirty (something that usability research often ignores in small-scale testing) and extreme scenarios that highlight risks and rare, but critical, usage patterns.

——————————————————————————————————

- **Heterogeneous samples.** You select the widest range of people possible on the dimensions of greatest interest (e.g., you might choose people from many industries, countries, genders, and experience ranges).

For any type of user research, it is important to be explicit about your sampling method and its limitations and biases.

THE USE OF INCENTIVES

Incentives can increase response rates to recruiting requests under some conditions, but this often requires approval of funds and possible legal reviews. So you should decide whether you are planning any extrinsic incentives (e.g., gift certificates, money, coupons, books, or other tangible gifts) early in the planning process so you have time to settle the financial and legal issues. Some issues to consider when you are thinking about extrinsic incentives for your interview study include the following (Dillman, Smyth, & Christian, 2009):

- **Will your participants be allowed to accept the incentives?** Government agencies, vendors, and some regulated industries may not permit any form of incentive for their employees. On the other hand, in certain cultures, token gifts are a business requirement.
- **Should you provide everyone with a small incentive (e.g., $10 gift certificate) versus offering a chance at a much larger incentive (e.g., an iPad®)?** There are a few issues here about offering a "chance at a reward." Conducting a drawing for a prize is a complex process in the United States because of different state and country regulations for drawings and sweepstakes. If you are planning a drawing where a small sample of participants will win a prize of some kind, consult a lawyer, especially if the drawing spans different states and countries.
- **Should you consider larger incentives with more complex surveys?** Dillman (2007, pp. 314–319) reports on a case study where an incentive for a large study increased response rates. From an exchange perspective, giving people more incentives for longer or more complex surveys seems equitable. However, large incentives might also indicate that the survey will be a lot of work and dissuade potential respondents from signing up.
- **What kind of incentives would you need if you are looking for doctors and research chemists or others for a focus group or interview?** You may need a substantial incentive to get people in some professions to participate in your study. The incentives must be appropriate for your participants and culture. Professional recruiters can provide recommendations on the amount. Incentives for many focus groups or interviews can run from $75 to $200. When considering the level of incentives, you should consider the cost of recruiting. The use of incentives may reduce the amount of time that your recruiter spends convincing people to attend your session. Incentives can include the following:
  a. Cash
  b. Gift certificates
  c. Gifts of hardware or software
  d. Donations in a person's name to a charity.

Keep in mind that some participants may not be allowed to accept gifts because they work for regulated or government organizations. Participants from financial organizations that are regulated, for example, often cannot accept any remuneration for their time.

Would Anyone Attend If There Was No Tangible Incentive?

The answer to this question is "maybe." If the subject of the focus group or interview is going to have a direct impact on the person or his or her organization or cause, then you might get people without providing any type of direct material or financial incentive. For example, if you are developing a software product and the participants are aware of the connection between your study and requirements for the next generation of the product, you may have sufficient intrinsic motivation to get the appropriate participants. If you are planning a focus group you could entice them with money or goods or you could provide a very good dinner (which sometimes is easier to do in corporate environments than giving money). One thing to keep in mind is that focus groups are now strongly linked with incentives (Morgan, 1998), so trying to get people to attend without incentives requires motivated participants.

- **What can you do if you have no funds for incentives or rewards?** If you have no money for incentives, you can consider other ways to persuade the person to participate. Here are several ways to persuade people to be part of your interview:
  a. You can explain how the interview results will benefit the participant. For example, you might conduct an interview to assess how to prioritize requirements to provide capabilities that are really needed by the user.
  b. You can ask for help and invoke what social psychologists call the norm of social responsibility.
  c. You can show trust and positive regard (Thibaut & Kelley, 1959) by personally addressing e-mail or paper invitations (don't address an invitation as the "Acme Usability Team" for example, use your real name), providing a phone number and e-mail, and using positive phrases like "Thanks for your help."
  d. You might indicate that the participant was chosen as a part of an elite group to provide feedback on an important topic.
  e. You can offer to provide feedback, for example, a report or an e-mail that summarizes the results.

●●●───

Be Careful about Promises to Provide Feedback!

Providing your participants with feedback requires some careful thought. On the surface, "provide feedback" sounds like a user-centered best practice and a way to build trust. However, sharing the results of surveys requires extra time to craft a report, and sometimes you may promise feedback and then find that the data from the surveys is politically sensitive or something that a competitor might use. If you are surveying from a captive group such as a user panel that has signed nondisclosures, feedback in the form of a summary report or brief letter might build trust and serve as an incentive to continue in the panel, but this can also have a negative impact if the users don't see any changes over the course of several years. For example, your structured survey to a user panel might ask users to rank their top five issues with a product. After a few years of listing the same issues and seeing no change to a product, those users might start to feel like your company isn't listening even though they do surveys and interviews often.

───

BIBLIOGRAPHY

Bailey, K. D. (1994). *Methods of social research* (4th ed.). New York, NY: The Free Press.

Barrett, J., & Herriotts, P. (2003). Running focus groups with older participants. In J. Langford, & D. McDonagh (Eds.), *Focus groups: Supporting effective product development* (pp. 63–72). London: Taylor and Francis.

Barrett, J., & Kirk, S. (2000). Running focus groups with elderly and disabled elderly participants. *Applied Ergonomics, 31,* 621–629.

Bernard, R. (2006). *Research methods in anthropology (4th ed.).* Lanham, MD: AltaMira Press.

Blankenship, A., Breen, G., & Dutka, A. (1998). *State of the art marketing research* (2nd ed.). Chicago, IL: NTC Business Books.

Bly, S. (1997). Field work: Is it product work? *Interactions, 4*(1), 25–30.

Bourque, L. B., & Fielder, E. P. (2003a). *How to conduct self-administered and mail surveys.* Thousand Oaks, CA: Sage Publications.

Bourque, L. B., & Fielder, E. P. (2003b). *How to conduct telephone surveys.* Newbury Park, CA: Sage Publications.

Bruseberg, A., & McDonagh, D. (2003). Focus groups in new product development: Designers' perspectives. In J. Langford, & D. McDonagh (Eds.), *Focus groups: Supporting effective product development* (pp. 63–72). London: Taylor and Francis.

Bryman, A. (2004). *Social research methods* (2nd ed.). Oxford, UK: Oxford University Press.

Butler, M. B. (1996). Getting to know your users: Usability roundtables at Lotus development. *interactions, 3*(1), 23–30.

Cannell, C. F., Fowler, F. J., & Marquis, K. H. (1968). The influence of interviewer and respondent psychological and behavioral variables on the reporting in household interviews. *Vital and Health Statistics, 26*(2), i-65.

Converse, J. M., & Presser, S. (1986). *Survey questions: Handcrafting the standardized questionnaire.* Beverly Hills, CA: Sage Publications. Sage University paper series on quantitative applications in the social sciences, series no. 07-063.

Coughlin, P., & Sklar, A. (2003). Bringing real world context into the focus group setting. In J. Langford, & D. McDonagh (Eds.), *Focus groups: Supporting effective product development.* London: Taylor & Francis.

Denning, S. (2004). *IDEO revolutionizes innovation and design with storytelling.* Retrieved on October 24, 2013 from: <http://www.stevedenning.com/Storytelling-in-the-News/144-ideo-story-telling-innovation.aspx>.

Denscombe, M. (2010). *The good research guide for small-scale social research* (4th ed.). Buckingham, UK: Open University Press.

Dillman, D. A. (1978). *Mail and phone surveys: The total design method.* New York, NY: Wiley.

Dillman, D. A. (2000). *Mail and internet surveys: The total design method* (2nd ed.). New York, NY: Wiley.

Dillman, D. A. (2007). *Mail and internet surveys: The tailored design method* (3rd ed.). Hoboken, NJ: Wiley.

Dillman, D. A., Smyth, J. D., & Christian, L. M. (2009). *Internet, mail, and mixed-mode surveys: The tailored design method* (3rd ed.). New York, NY: Wiley.

Dumas, J., & Redish, J. (1999). *A practical guide to usability testing (revised ed.)*. Exeter, UK: Intellect.

Fowler, F. J., Jr. (1993). *Survey research methods* (2nd ed.). Newbury Park, CA: Sage Publications.

Fowler, F. J., Jr. (1995). *Improving survey questions: Design and evaluation*. Newbury Park, CA: Sage Publications. Applied social research methods series, Vol. 38.

Fowler, F. J., Jr., & Mangione, T. W. (1990). *Standardized survey interviewing: Minimizing interview-related error*. Newbury Park, CA: Sage Publications. Applied social research methods series, Vol. 18.

Goldstein, N. J., Martin, S. J., & Cialdini, R. B. (2008). *Yes!: 50 scientifically proven ways to be persuasive*. New York, NY: The Free Press.

Goodwin, K. (2009). *Designing for the digital age: How to create human-centered products and services*. Indianapolis, IN: Wiley.

Greenbaum, T. (1993). The handbook for focus group research (revised ed.). Lexington, MA: Lexington Books.

Groves, R. M., & Kahn, R. L. (1979). *Surveys by telephone: A national comparison with personal interviews*. New York, NY: Academic Press.

Hackos, J. T., & Redish, J. C. (1998). *User and task analysis for interface design*. New York, NY: Wiley.

Hass, C. (2004). Using chat to conduct focus groups for disabled users. *Personal communication*.

Honold, P. (1999). Focus groups: A qualitative method to elicit culture-specific user requirements. In Hans-Jörg Bullinger, & J. Ziegler (Eds.), *Proceedings of the HCI international '99 (eighth international conference on human–computer interaction) on human–computer interaction: Communication, cooperation, and application design* (Vol. 2, pp. 3–7). Hillsdale, NJ, USA: Lawrence Erlbaum Associates Inc.

Howard S., Carroll J., Murphy J., & Peck J. (2002). Using 'endowed props' in scenario-based design. *Proceedings of the second Nordic conference on human–computer interaction*, October 2002.

James, J. M., & Bolstein, R. (1992). Large monetary incentives and their effect on mail survey response rates. *Public Opinion Quarterly, 56*, 442–453.

Jansen, A., Sulmon, N., Maarten Van Mechelen, M., Zaman, B., Vanattenhoven, J., & De Grooff, Dirk (2013). *Beyond the familiar?: exploring extreme input in brainstorms* (1347-1352). *In* CHI '13 Extended Abstracts on Human Factors in Computing Systems *(CHI EA '13)*. New York, NY, USA: ACM.

Jarrett, C., & Gaffney, G. (2009). *Forms that work: Designing web forms for usability*. Burlington, MA: Morgan Kaufmann.

Kidd, P., & Parshall, M. (2000). Getting the focus and the group: Enhancing analytical rigor in focus group research. *Qualitative Health Research, 10*(3), 293–308.

Kiley, D. (2005). *Shoot the focus group*. Retrieved on October 24, 2013 from <http://www.businessweek.com/stories/2005-11-13/shoot-the-focus-group>.

Krueger, R. A. (1998). *Moderating focus groups*. Thousand Oaks, CA: Sage Publications.

Krueger, R. A., & Casey, M. A. (2000). *Focus groups: A practical guide for applied research* (3rd ed.). Thousand Oaks, CA: Sage.

Kuniavsky, M. (2003). *Observing the user experience*. San Francisco, CA: Morgan Kaufmann.

Kvale, S. (1996). *Interviews: An introduction to qualitative research interviewing.* Thousand Oaks, CA: Sage.

Langford, J., & McDonagh, D. (Eds.), (2003). Focus groups: Supporting effective product development London, London and New York: Taylor and Francis.

Lavrakas, P. J. (1993). *Telephone survey methods: Sampling, Selection, and supervision* (2nd ed.). Newbury Park, CA: Sage Publications.

Levy, P. S., & Lemeshow, S. (1999). *Sampling of populations: Methods and applications* (3rd ed.). New York, NY: Wiley.

Mann, C., & Stewart, F. (2000). *Internet communication and qualitative research: A handbook for researching online.* London: Sage.

Merton, R, Fiske, K., & Kendall, P. L. (1956). *The focused interview: A manual of problems and procedures.* Glencoe, IL: The Free Press.

Merton, R, Fiske, K., & Kendall, P. L. (1990). *The focused interview: A manual of problems and procedures* (2nd ed.). Glencoe, IL: The Free Press.

Morgan, D. L. (1997). *Focus groups as qualitative research* (2nd ed.). Thousand Oaks, CA: Sage.

Morgan, D. L. (1998). *Planning focus groups (focus group kit 2).* Thousand Oaks, CA: Sage.

Nielsen, J. (1997). *The use and misuse of focus groups.* Retrieved October 24, 2013 from <http://www.nngroup.com/articles/focus-groups/>.

Nisbett, R. E., & Wilson, T. D. (1977). Telling more than we can know: Verbal reports on mental processes. *Psychological Review, 84,* 231–259.

Nokia. (2004). *Group testing: The best of both worlds.* Retrieved on November 9, 2004, from <http://www.forum.nokia.com/html_reader/main/1,4997,4480,00.html?page_nbr=2>.

O'Donnell, P. J., Scobie, G. E. W., & Baxter, I. (1991). The use of focus groups as an evaluation technique in HCI. In D. Diaper, & H. Hammond (Eds.), *People and computers VI* (pp. 211–224). Proceedings of the HCI '91 conference. Cambridge, UK: Cambridge University Press.

Olson, K., & Peytchev, A. (2007). Effect of Interviewer experience on interview pace and interviewer attitudes. *Public Opinion Quarterly, 71*(2), 273–286.

Payne, S. L. (1951). *The art of asking questions.* Princeton, NJ: Princeton University Press.

Pink, D. H. (2003). *Out of the box.* Retrieved October 24, 2013, from <http://www.fastcompany.com/47383/out-box>.

Preece, J., Rogers, Y., & Sharp, H. (2002). *Interaction design: Beyond human–computer interaction.* New York, NY: Wiley.

Ratner, J. (2003). Learning about the user experience on the web with the phone usability method. In J. Ratner (Ed.), *Human factors in web development* (pp. 123–146). Mahwah, NJ: Lawrence Erlbaum Associates Inc.

Robson, C. (2002). *Real world research* (2nd ed.). Malden, MA: Blackwell Publishing.

Rogers, W. A., Gilbert, D. K. & Cabrera, E. F. (1994). An in-depth analysis of automatic teller machine usage by older adults. *Proceedings of the human factors and ergonomics society 37th annual meeting.* Santa Monica, CA: Human Factors and Ergonomics Society.

Rogers, W. A., Gilbert, D. K., & Cabrera, E. F. (1997). An analysis of automatic teller machine usage by older adults: A structured interview approach. *Applied Ergonomics, 28,* 173–1 80.

Rosenbaum, S., Cockton, G., Coyne, K., Muller, M., & Rauch, T. (2002). Focus groups in HCI: Wealth of information or waste of resources? *In CHI '02 extended abstracts on human factors in computing systems* (pp. 702–703). Minneapolis, MN, April 20–25, 2002. New York, NY: ACM Press.

Salvador, T., & Howells, K. (1998, April). *Focus troupe: Using drama to create common context for new product concept end-user evaluations* (pp. 251–252). CHI '98, April 18–23, 1998.

Sato, S., & Salvador, T. (1999). Playacting and focus troupes: Theater techniques for creating quick, intense, immersive, and engaging focus group sessions. *Interactions 6*(5), 35–41.

Schensul, S. L., Schensul, J. J., & LeCompte, M. D. (1999). *Essential ethnographic methods: Observations, interviews, and questionnaires.* Walnut Creek, CA: AltaMira Press.

Schuman, H., & Presser, S. (1981). *Questions and answers in attitude surveys.* New York, NY: Academic Press.

Schuman, H., & Presser, S. (1996). *Questions and answers in attitude surveys.* London: Sage.

Shuy, R. W. (2001). In-person versus phone interviewing. In J. F. Bugrium, & H. A. Holstein (Eds.), *Handbook of interview research: Context & method* (pp. 537–555). Thousand Oaks: CA: Sage Publications.

Shuy, R. W. (2002). In-person versus Telephone Interviewing. In Gubrium, & Holstein (Eds.), *Handbook of interview research: Context & Method.* (pp. 537–557). Thousand Oaks: Sage.

Snyder, C. (2003). *Paper prototyping: The fast and easy way to define and refine user interfaces.* San Francisco, CA: Morgan Kaufmann.

Stewart, D. W., Shamdasani, P. N., & Rook, D. W. (2007). *Focus groups: Theory and practice* (2nd ed., Applied social research methods series, Vol. 20). Thousand Oaks, CA: Sage Publications. Applied social research methods series, Vol. 20.

Tamler, H. (1998). *How (much) to intervene in a usability testing session.* Retrieved October 24, 2013 from <http://www.htamler.com/papers/intervene/>.

Tatsuno, S. M. (1990). *Created in Japan: From imitators to world-class innovators.* New York, NY: Harper & Row.

Thibaut, J. W., & Kelley, H. H. (1959). *The social psychology of groups.* New York: Wiley.

Weiss, R. S. (1994). Learning from strangers: The art and method of qualitative *interview* studies. New York, NY: The Free Press.

Weller, S. C. (1998). Structured interviewing and questionnaire construction. In H. Russell Bernard (Ed.), *Handbook of methods in cultural anthropology* (pp. 365–410). Walnut Creek, CA: AltaMira Press.

Wilson, C. (2008). *Using the monetary method during a focus group.* Autodesk University exercise at the 2008 conference.

Wood, L. (1997). Semi-structured interviewing for user-centered design. *Interactions, 4*(2), 48–61.